Seek Ye First

A Study of the Kingdom of God

J S Blackburn

Scripture Truth Publications

SEEK YE FIRST

Based on articles in the magazine "Scripture Truth" 1967-70.

Hardback edition first published in May 1979 by Central Bible Hammond Trust Limited, Wooler.

Transferred to Digital Printing 2007

ISBN: 978-0-901860-61-3 (paperback)

ISBN: 978-0-901860-02-6 (hardback)

© Copyright 1978 J S Blackburn

A publication of Scripture Truth

All rights reserved. No part of this publication may be reproduced, stored in a retrieval system, or transmitted, in any form or by any means, electronic, mechanical, photocopying, recording or otherwise without prior permission of Scripture Truth Publications.

Scripture quotations, unless otherwise indicated, are taken from The Authorized (King James) Version. Rights in the Authorized Version are vested in the Crown. Reproduced by permission of the Crown's patentee, Cambridge University Press.

Cover photograph ©iStockphoto.com/earthmandala

Published by Scripture Truth Publications
Coopies Way, Coopies Lane,
Morpeth, Northumberland, NE61 6JN

Scripture Truth is an imprint of Central Bible Hammond Trust, a charitable trust

Printed and bound by Lightning Source

CONTENTS

		Page
1	Priorities	2
2	Understanding the Scriptures	6
3	'The Time is Fulfilled'	10
4	'The God of Heaven'	18
5	Some Questions about the Millennium	25
6	The Sermon on the Mount	31
7	The Mysteries of the Kingdom	38
8	The Parable of the Sower	43
9	Preaching the Word	50
10	Evil in the Kingdom	64
11	The Treasure and the Pearl	71
12	The Net Cast into the Sea	77
13	The Kingdom of Heaven and the Church	81
14	The Transfiguration	89
15	The Olivet Discourse	97
16	The Kingdom in the Epistles	105
17	'Occupy till I Come'	112
	Appendix	120
	Index of Subjects	123
	Index of Scriptures	128

LUKE 12: 13 - 31

13 And one of the company said unto him, Master, speak to my brother,
14 that he divide the inheritance with me. And he said unto him, Man,
15 who made me a judge or a divider over you? And he said unto them, Take heed, and beware of covetousness: for a man's life consisteth not
16 in the abundance of the things which he possesseth. And he spake a parable unto them, saying, The ground of a certain rich man brought
17 forth plentifully: And he thought within himself, saying, What shall I
18 do, because I have no room where to bestow my fruits? And he said, This will I do: I will pull down my barns, and build greater; and there
19 will I bestow all my fruits and my goods. And I will say to my soul, Soul, thou hast much goods laid up for many years; take thine ease, eat,
20 drink, and be merry. But God said unto him, Thou fool, this night thy soul shall be required of thee: then whose shall those things be, which
21 thou hast provided? So is he that layeth up treasure for himself, and is
22 not rich toward God. And he said unto his disciples, Therefore I say unto you, Take no thought for your life, what ye shall eat; neither for
23 the body, what ye shall put on. The life is more than meat, and the
24 body is more than raiment. Consider the ravens: for they neither sow nor reap; which neither have storehouse nor barn; and God feedeth
25 them: how much more are ye better than the fowls? And which of you
26 with taking thought can add to his stature one cubit? If ye then be not able to do that thing which is least, why take ye thought for the rest?
27 Consider the lilies how they grow: they toil not, they spin not; and yet I say unto you, that Solomon in all his glory was not arrayed like one
28 of these. If then God so clothe the grass, which is today in the field, and tomorrow is cast into the oven; how much more will he clothe you,
29 O ye of little faith? And seek not ye what ye shall eat, or what ye shall
30 drink, neither be ye of doubtful mind. For all these things do the nations of the world seek after: and your Father knoweth that ye have
31 need of these things. But rather seek ye the kingdom of God; and all these things shall be added unto you.

Chapter 1

PRIORITIES

No request could be more topical than that with which this passage opens, "Master, speak to my brother, that he divide the inheritance with me." Not only is it topical in the time and place in which these words are being written, but it is difficult to imagine any time to come, short of the coming of the Kingdom of God on earth, when the request will be any less topical than it is today. It seems to say, "a finite amount of this world's good is available, and I want a larger share for myself."

Two questions dominate the life of nations. There is the problem of the size of the national income, or of the nation's wealth — an industrial and economic question; and there is the social and political question of sharing it justly. The great divide between contemporary east and west is their divergence on these points. The east, in general, has settled for some form of communism. The west in general regards this as the greatest possible danger. All the disputes about Marxism and all the strikes in every land are forms in which this grievance is constantly recurring.

A most challenging and reassuring fact for every Christian is that such a question was put to the Master and that we know His answers. "Master", said the man-in-the-street, "speak to my brother that he divide the inheritance with me." We have this cry from the heart of every have-not, be it man or nation. The Master's answer was, "Man, who made me a judge or a divider over you?" — which, being interpreted, means, "Man, I am not here to settle such questions — not yet." We must note how necessary it is to add "not yet". The Father has committed all judgment into the hands of the Son. In the day of His power He will indeed be the judge and the supreme arbiter. It is a basic fact about the whole lapse of time up to Christ's appearing, that the time of His judgment is not yet. At His first coming God was in Christ, "not imputing their trespasses unto them". The Christian's confidence is not that these problems in industry, commerce and economics are not important, but that they will not receive a just and complete solution until Christ's Kingdom comes, *and* that for the Christian, the top priority lies elsewhere.

What follows is clearly to be divided into two paragraphs. From v.15

"He spake to the company" of which the questioner was one. From v.22 He explicitly addressed His disciples, and we must clearly distinguish the two kinds of living, the two outlooks on the world. Both attitudes encompass the need for food, for clothing, for a treasure for the heart. On the one hand there is the life of those who give top priority to planning the abundance of their possessions and who leave God out of the calculation. On the other hand there are the disciples of Christ, who, peaceful in the knowledge of the care of their Father in heaven, give first priority to His Kingdom.

From v.15 the Lord attributes the question to covetousness, and enforces the point with the story of the rich man who was yet, in the last analysis, a fool. The essentials of the story lie in two contrasts, which underline the fact that God was not in all his thoughts. He said to himself and of himself, "much goods"; but God said, "not rich". He said to himself and of himself, "many years"; but God said, "this night". He was in fact not right with God, and all his planning came to less than nothing. These are exactly the thoughts of the world we live in. Every conversation heard, every placard, every broadcast, drums into our minds the thinking, the planning, the values of a world like this, and therefore we need the Lord's voice to teach us the last word, the epitaph, on such living. "A man's life consisteth not in the abundance of the things which he possesseth".

From v.22 the Lord addresses His disciples, and the key-phrase of the message is, "Take no thought". The meaning of this phrase in formal English is, "Do not be anxious", and in colloquial English, "Don't worry". And this is not the mere catch-phrase it is in modern speech, for we are provided with (1) facts for the heart which dispel worry, (2) something better to do, (3) the Lord's command which is its own enabling. It would be difficult to prove that the dangers of anxiety are greater today than ever before, but few would doubt that they are in fact greater due to the accelerated pace of modern life and the complexity of the problems which beset the world. Wider dissemination of the knowledge of these problems is not the least part of the cause of the modern malaise. The Bible has a good deal to say about worry, but in order to see this, we have to disencumber the A.V. of some confusion in translation. Apart from Luke 12, the two best known passages are Philippians 4:6 and 1 Peter 5:7. Colloquially they would be translated, "Don't worry about anything", and "Rolling off all your worry on to Him". We are thus confronted with one of the commandments of the Lord, once from the lips of the Master Himself, once through the words of Paul, and again through the mouth of Peter. None obeys this commandment with completeness, but we must allow its power to come upon us constantly. The next thing to be noted is that in no case is this a mere prohibition, a negative. In each case the means are given to enable us to overcome evil with good. Peter accompanies the command with the comforting assurance, "He careth for you". Paul joins immediately the command to put in its place prayer — "but in every thing by prayer and supplication with thanksgiving let your requests be made known unto God". Then comes the promise joined to the prayer, "And the peace of God, which passeth all understanding, shall keep your hearts and minds through Christ Jesus."

Here in Luke 12 a much more extended discourse deals with the facts for the heart which dispel worry. It agrees exactly, however, with Peter's antidote, and might be summarised, *"God is taking care of you".* The disciples are asked to consider the ravens and the lilies. The lesson to be learned is focused at a single point, that God takes care of them. We are not to imitate the ravens in their abstinence from planned labour, nor the lilies in the magnificence of their clothing. We are to take account of the fact that God feeds and clothes His creatures. Scripture in other places enforces the necessity of labour on our part, and in others yet the avoidance of magnificent raiment, but here, one thing only is taught. Even taking account of all our labour, it is God who feeds His children, and all our toiling and spinning would not equal the splendour with which God clothes the lilies. G.K. Chesterton has a striking passage on v.28. "If then God so clothe the grass, which is today in the field, and tomorrow is cast into the oven; how much more will he clothe you, O ye of little faith?" "Even in the matter of literary style, if we suppose ourselves sufficiently detached to look at it in that light, there is a curious quality...of piling tower upon tower...making a pagoda of degrees like the seven heavens...There is perhaps nothing so perfect in all language or literature as the use of these three degrees in the parable of the lilies of the field; in which He seems first to take one small flower in His hand and note its simplicity and even its impotence; then suddenly expands it in flamboyant colours into all the palaces and pavilions full of a great name in national glory; and then, by yet a third overturn, shrivels it to nothing once more with a gesture as if throwing it away...and if God so clothes the grass that today is and tomorrow is cast into the oven — how much more.."

If vv.22 to 28 tell us what to avoid (together with the antidote — trust in God's care expressed in prayer), vv.29 to 31 tell what to *do*, what is the practical enterprise into which our energies are to be flung, in fearless abandon of anxiety as to earthly cares, the Kingdom of God. In this context, to seek something is to toil and sow for it, and the all-embracive object of the Christian's toil is the Kingdom of God. The whole tenor of Scripture leads us to read these words as the great statement of the disciple's *priorities.* We are obviously to take action about food and clothing and the earthly needs of this life, but seeking these things is not the disciple's first priority. There are other words of Scripture which require a parallel interpretation. Paul's confession in 2 Corinthians 4:18 is "While we look not at the things which are seen, but at the things which are not seen: for the things which are seen are temporal; but the things which are not seen are eternal". He did not, and could not ignore the things which are seen — in the context, his troubles, but he did not decide his life's course by taking account of the seen things. His gaze was fixed on the eternal things, and it was in taking account of these that his life's course was determined. They were his first priority. The word 'seek' appears also in Colossians 3:1. "Seek those things which are above", and this is accompanied by the injunction, "Mind things above, not things on earth". It is obviously necessary that Christians should mind things on earth, and anyone could enumerate Scriptures which instruct them to do so; but things on earth are not to dominate us. They are not to be our first priority. Our first priority is to be "things which are above, where Christ sitteth on the right hand of God". The matter of priorities is very clear in 1 Timothy 4:8; "Bodily exercise profiteth for a little: but godliness is profitable unto all things, having promise of the life that now is, and of that which is to come".

Of all these, and other terms in which the Christian's priorities are presented, perhaps the first is the most fundamental and inclusive. In Matthew's terms it reads "Seek ye first the kingdom of God". The Kingdom of God is the Christian's first priority. Into this enterprise he is to pour the first of his prayers, the finest of his energies, and the best of his time. It is indeed worth while to enquire what is this Kingdom which should loom so large in terms of practical life, and it is to this question that we now address ourselves.

Chapter 2

UNDERSTANDING THE SCRIPTURES

The first chapter drew attention to the dominant importance of the Kingdom of God for life and work, but it is now necessary to look at the place the Kingdom occupies in the New Testament in general, and therefore its importance for doctrine, that is, for an enlightened understanding of Scripture. It is not possible to be right in understanding Scripture, unless we take proper account of a subject which figures so largely in it. The examination now to be entered on will in addition serve to underline the fact that practical issues are so frequently clinched by reference to the Kingdom of God.

The Synoptic Gospels, as distinct from the Gospel of John, present the Kingdom of God as one of their main themes. The fullest treatment is, of course, that of the Kingdom of heaven in Matthew, though there are weighty pronouncements in the other gospels which will be noted in due course. Almost a quarter of the total bulk of the Gospel of Matthew is occupied by three great discourses. The first, generally called the Sermon on the Mount, occupies chapters five, six and seven. In this discourse the King proclaims the principles and laws of His Kingdom. The second fills chapter thirteen, in which the King sets out by parables the Mysteries of His Kingdom, that is its history in its present form. The third is found in chapters twenty-four and twenty-five, and in it the King discloses what His disciples needed to know about the future of the Kingdom: the future for Israel in chapter twenty-four, for Christ's servants and disciples in chapter twenty-five to verse 30, and for the Gentile nations in twenty-five, vv.31 to 46.

Thus in the Synoptic Gospels we find recorded the teaching of the Lord Jesus which encompasses the whole sweep of Kingdom truth. Does this aspect of truth fade out of sight as Church truth and practice is developed? Indeed it does not, and in the Acts we must not fail to see that it still forms a staple of the instruction given by the Risen Lord and by the great apostle. How precious in the recollections of the disciples must have been the forty days which they passed in fellowship with the Lord, alive after His passion by many infallible proofs. We have the story of the first resurrection day in great detail. The appearance to the devoted women who came to the sepulchre in the grey dawn; His dealings with the travellers on the Emmaus road, causing their hearts to burn within them while He opened to them in all the Scriptures the things concerning Himself; His appearing in the midst of His own gathered together behind closed doors for fear of the Jews and their gladness when they knew Him. All this, and more, comes to mind as we go over the details of that first Lord's day. And as the story proceeds, we can by piecing together the various parts learn about the recovery of those out of the way, the opening of their understanding, their commissioning for the time of His absence, and the promise of power from on high, the gift and coming of the Holy Spirit. Then in Acts 1:3 the words occur "appearing unto them by the space of forty days and speaking the things concerning the kingdom of God". The words plainly mean that this theme, the Kingdom of God, formed the subject of His discussions during the forty days between His resurrection and His ascension. Was this theme additional to the others we have reviewed; the interpretation of the things in all the Scriptures concerning Himself, the great commission, the gift of the Spirit, His second coming and the end of the age? I think not. It would be difficult so to read Acts 1:3. A far more natural meaning would be that these things were themselves the "things pertaining to the kingdom of God". The Kingdom of God was not an additional theme, but these themes so moving to the hearts of the disciples were themselves the constituent parts of the wider subject. We should misconceive the Kingdom of God if we were to think of it as a compartment of truth separate from these others. In some important sense the Kingdom of God was the all-inclusive theme embracing in its sweep all these other details of instruction. Thus it is suggested that the Kingdom of God is the theme with which the Lord occupied the thoughts of His own after His resurrection.

Few would doubt that there is a special, almost symbolical, meaning to be attached to the detail of Paul's ministry in connection with Ephesus, and from this point of view the mention of Ephesus leads us to the pinnacle of New Testament truth as unfolded in the epistle bearing that name. It is customary to analyse the Acts by reference to the journeys of the apostle, the first, the second, and the third. While the first journey may well be a unit of special significance in the mind of the Spirit, there are few things more plain than that the second and third journeys are not so. In the later chapters of Acts it appears far more likely that in the mind of the Spirit in the structure of the narrative, the units of significance are the cities, to which the apostle addressed letters. Paul embarks on his second journey as recorded in 15:40, and from that point the narrative divisions are events in Philippi (16:12-40), Thessalonica (17:1-9), Corinth (18:1-28), overlapping with Ephesus (18:24 to 19:41 and 20:17-38). The scope, detail, and explanation of the long section centred on Ephesus emphasise the importance attached to what took place in that city. The explanation is contained in the famous address to the Ephesian elders contained in the last passage quoted. In this discourse, leading, as has been noted, to the pinnacle of New Testament truth, the Kingdom of God is one of four themes epitomising Paul's teaching while he was labouring at the establishment of that church. Two of the four themes cover the message by which the hearers had been first brought into blessing. These two were "repentance toward God, and faith toward our Lord Jesus Christ", (v.21) and "the gospel of the grace of God" (v.24). The remaining two themes form the message by which those brought into blessing were established and built up: "the kingdom of God" (v.25), and "all the counsel of God" (v.27). Here again, it appears most likely that the last two expressions quoted cover the whole range of establishing truth, the Kingdom of God from the point of view of the Christian's responsibility, and the whole counsel of God from the point of view of God's immutable will and purpose. Thus, although special care may be needed to understand the expression aright, the important place given to the Kingdom of God in Acts 20 gives the theme a lasting relevance throughout the present era.

At the close of the Acts Paul is found (on the same page as the Epistle to the Romans begins) at Rome spending a whole day with the chief Jews. In vv.23 and 31 the themes of the conference are stated. They are, first, testifying and teaching the Kingdom of God, and second, persuading and teaching the things concerning Jesus.

In the Epistles there are important references to the Kingdom of God in Romans, 1 Corinthians (three or four), Galatians, Ephesians, Colossians, 1 and 2 Thessalonians. These references may readily be grouped by certain concepts. The first is the phrase: "the kingdom of God is...", and such passages describe the nature of the Kingdom. (Romans 14:17, 1 Corinthians 4:20). The second group contains the phrase: " inherit the kingdom of God" (1 Corinthians 6:9, 10; 15:50, Galatians 5:21, Ephesians 5:5). This expression probably indicates that the context specifies the character and behaviour of those who will and will not receive rewards in the Kingdom as it will be established in power at the Second Advent. The third phrase is: "unto the kingdom of God", (Colossians 4:11, 1 Thessalonians 2:12), and draws attention to certain actions which will have results in the future Kingdom. There is one reference to those who will be "counted worthy of the kingdom of God" (2 Thessalonians 1:5).

Finally, in the Revelation (12:10), "Now is come...the kingdom of our God" is the theme celebrated in heaven. With so voluminous a stream of teaching and truth running through the New Testament, and leading to such a conclusion, how can we fail to appreciate the necessity of giving a just place to the theme of the Kingdom of God in the scheme of divine truth, in its bearing on the Christian's behaviour and responsibility, as distinct from the viewpoint of God's counsel and purpose, but always in view of the lordship of Christ. And this outlook carries with it in full measure what is required to satisfy the heart, for "the kingdom of God is not meat and drink; but righteousness, and peace, and joy in the Holy Ghost".

MARK 1: 14, 15.

14 Now after that John was put in prison, Jesus came into Galilee,
15 preaching the gospel of the kingdom of God, And saying, The time is fulfilled, and the kingdom of God is at hand: repent ye, and believe the gospel.

LUKE 7: 28.

28 For I say unto you, Among those that are born of women there is not a greater prophet than John the Baptist: but he that is least in the kingdom of God is greater than he.

LUKE 16: 16.

16 The law and the prophets were until John: since that time the kingdom of God is preached, and every man presseth into it.

Chapter 3

"THE TIME IS FULFILLED"

The Kingdom of God had no existence prior to New Testament times. This fact is of such fundamental importance that it is worth while to linger over it. It begins to emerge in the earliest references in the Gospels, and to bring this out more clearly, let us start with Mark 1:14 and 15. "Now after that John was put in prison, Jesus came into Galilee, preaching the gospel of the kingdom of God, And saying, The time is fulfilled, and the kingdom of God is at hand: repent ye, and believe the gospel".

There are here three announcements about the Kingdom of God. First, it is a gospel, that is, good news. Although it involves assuming beforehand what still remains to be demonstrated from Scripture, it is impossible not to pause at this point and reflect on the joy and gladness which comes with the certainty that God is going to reign on earth, that His will is going to be done on earth as it is in heaven. In no other way shall all "the crooked be made straight, and the rough ways shall be made smooth". Only when "out of Zion shall go forth the law, and the word of the Lord from Jerusalem" shall the nations "beat their swords into ploughshares and their spears into pruninghooks: nation shall not lift up sword against nation, neither shall they learn war any more". When God's Kingdom appears then His people will say, "Lo, this is our God; we have waited for Him...we will be glad and rejoice in His salvation". The best possible news regarding this earth is the gospel of God's Kingdom, even though that Kingdom must be established by the bringing down of all man's loftiness and the purging of his sin. The second announcement about the Kingdom of God in Mark 1:15 is, "the time is fulfilled". A definite time was coming to an end with this preaching. From the moment of His utterance in this verse, it was necessary to go back over a fixed period now fulfilled. Where shall we look to find a promise which would fit these circumstances? Surely we are taken directly to Daniel 2:44. "In the days of these kings shall the God of heaven set up a kingdom, which shall never be destroyed". We must return later to this Scripture in Daniel for a fuller examination, but for the time being we note that an earthly Kingdom of God and of heaven established in the Person of the Stone cut out without hands was promised to follow and displace the Roman Empire. *The primary meaning, therefore, of the phrase "the Kingdom of God" is the millennial reign of Christ.* Accordingly, the third announcement in Mark 1:15 is that the Kingdom of God is "at hand", and this is the principal part of the message. In Jesus the Kingdom of God with all its glowing promise had come near.

In Daniel 7:13, most explicitly amplified in Matthew 24:30, the Second Coming of Christ to establish the Kingdom of God in power would be an event like lightning, visible and compelling for all the tribes of the earth. Now, although the presence of the King was evidenced by samples of the powers of the world to come (Luke 10:11, "notwithstanding be ye sure of this, that the kingdom of God is come nigh unto you"), very soon the Lord began to explain to His disciples the very different manner in which the Kingdom was to be set up at that time. Its promised establishment by the visible splendour and power of His Second Coming was not a mystery. It was not something hitherto hidden and unrevealed. It was clearly described by Daniel. In all the Synoptic Gospels we have it recorded that Jesus began to initiate His disciples by parables into *the mysteries of the Kingdom, a hitherto unrevealed form of the Kingdom to precede the Millennium,* and at that moment being inaugurated by the quiet going forth of the Sower, sowing the seed of the Word of God. Reflection on the sweep of Kingdom truth reviewed in the previous chapter seems to make it plain that it is this mystery form of the Kingdom of God which is the predominant, though not the exclusive subject of the New Testament references.

The truth under consideration in this chapter is that the Kingdom of God had no existence before New Testament times, and further thought must be given to this. A popular view is that since God is the King eternal, He must always have had a Kingdom. That God is eternally and in all time the Sovereign Lord and Ruler of all is not in question, but it is absolutely indisputable that the phrase "the Kingdom of God" as used throughout the New Testament does *not* refer to this general, universal Kingdom of God in all time. It does not refer to God's general superintendence of history. It refers primarily to the millennial reign of Christ, but more often to the mystery form of that Kingdom which likewise had no existence before the Son of Man went forth as the Sower. Abraham and Moses and David and John the Baptist were not in the Kingdom of God, but the least professor of repentance and faith in Christ is in that Kingdom. This truth is quite categorically stated by the Lord in two passages: "There is not a greater prophet than John the Baptist: but he that is least in the kingdom of God is greater than he" (Luke 7:28). "The law and the prophets were until John: since that time the kingdom of God is preached" (Luke 16:16).

It is of course necessary to take patient account of other Scriptures which have often been quoted in this connection. Perhaps the two most important are 1 Chronicles 28:5 and Matthew 21:43. The former refers to the throne of David and Solomon as "the throne of the kingdom of Jehovah over Israel", and this concept is indeed one of great interest, setting in a wonderful light the true nature of David's kingdom and of God's blessing on the man after His own heart. But it is abundantly plain that the one – the throne of the kingdom of Jehovah over Israel – is at the beginning of the chain of events described in Daniel, while the other – the Kingdom of God over the whole earth (Daniel 2:35) – is at the end of the chain. There is a real connection, in that it was on account of the sad infidelity of the later kings of David's line that the glory departed and earthly dominion was given by God to Nebuchadnezzar. Only when the times of the Gentiles have run their course will a Kingdom far greater than David's appear – the Kingdom of God and of heaven.* Matthew 21:43 reads, in explanation of the parable of the wicked husbandmen, "Therefore say I unto you, The kingdom of God shall be taken from you, and given to a nation bringing forth the fruits thereof". This has been held to mean that Israel must have possessed the Kingdom of God before their rejection of Christ. In view, however, of the categorical nature of the Scriptures quoted above, which state so clearly that the Kingdom of God had no existence prior to New Testament times, Matthew 21:43 need mean no more than that the Kingdom of God was removed from being at hand, or near, for Israel.

The point we have reached in our study of the fact that only in the New Testament is the Kingdom of God set up, might well lead us to end in a meditation on the desire of God to receive fruit. In the Kingdom of God He does receive that fruit: what more moving appeal could reach us than this to "seek first the Kingdom of God". See how the heart of God is involved, and the heart of the prophet is awakened when he sings (Isaiah 5:1ff) "I will sing to my wellbeloved a song of my beloved touching his vineyard". Then, after detailing the manner in which nothing in the way of care and cultivation which could be lavished upon it had been withheld, Jehovah turns Himself and addresses His people, "I looked that it should bring forth grapes". Here is the heart of God, in patient love looking for response, for fruit to be His delight from the people of His choice: but "it brought forth wild grapes". The fruit was and is character and behaviour. The fruit He called wild grapes was oppression and injustice between brethren, self-indulgence, and pride.

Shall we not be the people bringing forth fruit for God? Shall we not seek first that Kingdom in which such fruit is found? In olden times, as He mourned over His vineyard, He broke down the wall thereof, and the wild boar from the forest wasted it, because this was the issue of a necessary probation. It was in the Gospel days that He took away His Kingdom and gave it to a people bringing forth its fruits. Make no mistake, God has not given up His deep desire to receive fruit from His people. Rather, He has, in the Kingdom of God, taken a new way to obtain it. The appointed instrument is the good seed of the word of God, and by the power of the Holy Spirit given, the fruit is seen: love, joy, peace, longsuffering, gentleness, goodness, faith, meekness, self-control.

Before finally closing this chapter, it seems desirable to deal with the relation between the two expressions, the Kingdom of God and the Kingdom

---

*That Kingdom will, of course, include the restoration of Israel, and of David's throne.

of heaven. The view taken in this book is that for most practical purposes they are indistinguishable. I have found it helpful to consider the statements often heard and read about alleged differences. It is commonly believed that a difference exists in that the Kingdom of God includes only what is real, while the Kingdom of heaven includes all persons professing faith in Christ. I think this belief is based on John 3:3 and 5, which say that only those born again can see or enter the Kingdom of God. If this passage stood alone, it could have this meaning, but since it does not stand alone, and since other words of the Saviour clearly state that the Kingdom of God includes more than what is real, we must understand that John 3:3 and 5 have another meaning, which is that what is real in the Kingdom of God must result from the new birth. It is analogous to other statements in John's writings, for instance, "Whosoever is born of God...cannot sin." Both passages must be understood in a particular sense.

It is to the parables in which both expressions occur that we must look for guidance on this point. The Kingdom of God and the Kingdom of heaven are interchangeable in the parable of the mustard seed (Matthew 13:31, 32 and Mark 4:30-32). Similarly in the parable of the leaven in the meal. Matthew 13:33, "The kingdom of heaven is like unto leaven, which a woman took, and hid in three measures of meal, till the whole was leavened." Luke 13:20,21, "The kingdom of God...is like leaven, which a woman took and hid in three measures of meal, till the whole was leavened." The meaning of these parables will be explained later, but it is indubitable from them that the Kingdom of God and the Kingdom of heaven both refer to a wider circle than that of true faith.

Again, it is commonly believed that the kingdom of God covers all history (as has been explained earlier in this chapter), while, on the other hand, the Kingdom of heaven is different in that it is a dispensational term, and belongs to the New Testament only. Here again, the passages already quoted to show that the Kingdom had no existence prior to New Testament times are exactly paralleled by others which name the Kingdom of heaven: Mark 1: '14 and 15 by Matthew 4: 17, "Jesus began to preach, and to say, Repent: for the kingdom of heaven is at hand." Luke 7:28 is paralleled by Matthew 11:11: "There hath not risen a greater than John the Baptist: notwithstanding he that is least in the kingdom of heaven is greater than he." Luke 16:16 on the Kingdom of God is paralleled by Matthew 11:12,13, on the Kingdom of heaven. From these parallels it is clear that both the Kingdom of God and the Kingdom of heaven began simultaneously, that is, when the law and the prophets, the Old Testament, were ended. John the Baptist is the dividing line for both.

That the Spirit of God intends some distinction in aspect by the use of the Kingdom of heaven in Matthew's gospel, we can scarcely doubt. Perhaps the most plausible suggestion is that Kingdom of heaven is the name given to the Kingdom of God during the period when the King is absent in heaven, and although this does not convince me, this view gives an occasional glimpse of itself in later chapters. Another possibility is that the distinct purpose of Matthew's Gospel requires the special use of the word 'heaven' arising from its being the Gospel to the Jews. 'Your Father which is in heaven' is also practically restricted to Matthew. If there is a distinction which affects the kind of study we have undertaken, then it is deeply hidden. On the surface the two expressions are synonymous. We ought also to take note of the five occurrences in Matthew of 'the kingdom of God'. (6:33, 12:28, 19:24, 21:31, 21:43). Of these one is of special interest in that it hints at another definition of the Kingdom of God. The story of the blasphemy of the Pharisees in attributing the Lord's miracles to Satan appears in Matthew 12:22 to 32. V. 28 reads: "if I cast out demons by the Spirit of God, then the kingdom of God is come unto you". The Kingdom of God might in this place be understood as the intervention of God's power for the deliverance of man from Satan's power. This definition would be by no means at variance with the meaning we have obtained from Daniel.

DANIEL 2: 31 - 45.

31 Thou, O king, sawest, and behold a great image. This great image, whose brightness was excellent, stood before thee; and the form thereof
32 was terrible. This image's head was of fine gold, his breast and his arms
33 of silver, his belly and his thighs of brass, His legs of iron, his feet part of
34 iron and part of clay. Thou sawest till that a stone was cut out without hands, which smote the image upon his feet that were of iron and clay,
35 and brake them to pieces. Then was the iron, the clay, the brass, the silver, and the gold, broken to pieces together, and became like the chaff of the summer threshingfloors; and the wind carried them away, that no place was found for them: and the stone that smote the image
36 became a great mountain, and filled the whole earth. This is the dream;
37 and we will tell the interpretation thereof before the king. Thou, O king, art a king of kings: for the God of heaven hath given thee a
38 kingdom, power, and strength, and glory. And wheresoever the children of men dwell, the beasts of the field and the fowls of the heaven hath he given into thine hand, and hath made thee ruler over them all. Thou
39 art this head of gold. And after thee shall arise another kingdom inferior to thee, and another third kingdom of brass, which shall bear
40 rule over all the earth. And the fourth kingdom shall be strong as iron: forasmuch as iron breaketh in pieces and subdueth all things: and as
41 iron that breaketh all these, shall it break in pieces and bruise. And whereas thou sawest the feet and toes, part of potters' clay, and part of iron, the kingdom shall be divided; but there shall be in it of the strength of the iron, forasmuch as thou sawest the iron mixed with
42 miry clay. And as the toes of the feet were part of iron, and part of clay,
43 so the kingdom shall be partly strong, and partly broken. And whereas thou sawest iron mixed with miry clay, they shall mingle themselves with the seed of men: but they shall not cleave one to another, even as iron is
44 not mixed with clay. And in the days of these kings shall the God of heaven set up a kingdom, which shall never be destroyed: and the kingdom shall not be left to other people, but it shall break in pieces and
45 consume all these kingdoms, and it shall stand for ever. Forasmuch as thou sawest that the stone was cut out of the mountain without hands, and that it brake in pieces the iron, the brass, the clay, the silver, and the gold; the great God hath made known to the king what shall come to pass hereafter: and the dream is certain, and the interpretation thereof sure.

DANIEL 7.

2 Daniel spake and said, I saw in my vision by night, and, behold, the
3 four winds of the heaven strove upon the great sea. And four great
4 beasts came up from the sea, diverse one from another. The first was like a lion, and had eagle's wings: I beheld till the wings thereof were plucked, and it was lifted up from the earth, and made stand upon the

5 feet as a man, and a man's heart was given to it. And behold another beast, a second, like to a bear, and it raised up itself on one side, and it had three ribs in the mouth of it between the teeth of it: and they
6 said thus unto it, Arise, devour much flesh. After this I beheld, and lo another, like a leopard, which had upon the back of it four wings of a
7 fowl; the beast had also four heads; and dominion was given to it. After this I saw in the night visions, and behold a fourth beast, dreadful and terrible, and strong exceedingly; and it had great iron teeth: it devoured and brake in pieces, and stamped the residue with the feet of it: and it was diverse from all the beasts that were before it; and it had ten horns.
8 I considered the horns, and, behold, there came up among them another little horn, before whom there were three of the first horns plucked up by the roots: and, behold, in this horn were eyes like the eyes of man, and a mouth speaking great things....
13 I saw in the night visions, and, behold, one like the Son of man came with the clouds of heaven, and came to the Ancient of days, and they
14 brought him near before him. And there was given him dominion, and glory, and a kingdom, that all people, nations, and languages, should serve him: his dominion is an everlasting dominion, which shall not pass away, and his kingdom that which shall not be destroyed....
17 These great beasts, which are four, are four kings, which shall arise out
18 of the earth. But the saints of the most High shall take the kingdom,
19 and possess the kingdom for ever, even for ever and ever. Then I would know the truth of the fourth beast, which was diverse from all the others, exceeding dreadful, whose teeth were of iron, and his nails of brass; which devoured, brake in pieces, and stamped the residue with
20 his feet; And of the ten horns that were in his head, and of the other which came up, and before whom three fell; even of that horn that had eyes, and a mouth that spake very great things, whose look was more
21 stout than his fellows. I beheld, and the same horn made war with the
22 saints, and prevailed against them; Until the Ancient of days came, and judgment was given to the saints of the most High; and the time came
23 that the saints possessed the kingdom. Thus he said, The fourth beast shall be the fourth kingdom upon earth, which shall be diverse from all kingdoms, and shall devour the whole earth, and shall tread it down,
24 and break it in pieces. And the ten horns out of this kingdom are ten kings that shall arise: and another shall rise after them; and he shall be
25 diverse from the first, and he shall subdue three kings. And he shall speak great words against the most High, and shall wear out the saints of the most High, and think to change times and laws: and they shall be
26 given into his hand until a time and times and the dividing of time. But the judgment shall sit and they shall take away his dominion, to
27 consume and to destroy it unto the end. And the kingdom and dominion, and the greatness of the kingdom under the whole heaven,

shall be given to the people of the saints of the most High, whose kingdom is an everlasting kingdom, and all dominions shall serve and obey him.

Chapter 4

"THE GOD OF HEAVEN SHALL SET UP A KINGDOM"

It has already been remarked that the expressions "the Kingdom of God" and "the Kingdom of heaven" find their origin in the Prophecy of Daniel. The leading passage has already been noted, Daniel 2:44, and closer study must now be given to this verse in its context, and also to the parallel in Daniel 7:18 and 27.

Daniel 2 forms part of the section in which God's revelations are not given to His people in the person of the prophet directly, but in a vision to the first Gentile king himself, Nebuchadnezzar, which is then interpreted by Daniel with wisdom imparted by God. It is thus to be expected that the view presented will be an external view of the course and succession of Gentile powers, rather than their character in the eyes of God, or their relations with His people Israel. The dream of Daniel 2 is part of God's discipline of Nebuchadnezzar, not involving the exercise of the prophet's spirit as do the later visions given to himself.

The dream of Nebuchadnezzar's image and its interpretation may be seen as "the story of the kingdoms". Nebuchadnezzar was seen to be a "king of kings", and with the kingdom given him was added "power and strength and glory". His kingdom was over other kings, and the whole earth as inhabited by men, beasts and fowls. Also, in his "kingdom" were included his Babylonian successors, and likewise for the second, third and fourth kingdoms.

Thus verse 39 speaks also of kingdoms, the second and the third, inferior to the first, yet ruling the whole earth. The fourth kingdom occupies verses 40 - 43, subduing all things, breaking in pieces and bruising, yet divided and adulterated in the end.

It will readily be observed that it is the word "kingdom" which dominates the passage, occurring six times in these few verses. We must try to grasp its bearing. It is not general or abstract in meaning. It signifies the actual historical rule of one person, with his hierarchy of servants and ministers as administrators over the whole habitable earth. It is a kingdom given by God, and in terms of the boldness of these children of God who withstood the king's decree, and the lessons subsequently enforced by the king's sentence to madness, such kingdoms are concrete expressions of the fact that the Most

High rules in the kingdoms of men, and disposes as He wills.

It is also most important to notice that according to Bible history, and prophecy prior to the book of Daniel, in Jerusalem was "the throne of the kingdom of Jehovah over Israel" (1 Chronicles 28:5). When Nebuchadnezzar became Jehovah's servant (Ezekiel 29:20 and 30:24-26) it was to take away that throne which from that moment ceased altogether from the earth, and in its place God gave to Nebuchadnezzar the splendid golden kingdom here described. Thus began the times of the Gentiles. Let us not fail to notice also the contrast between the throne of David and Solomon over Israel, and the kingdom of Nebuchadnezzar and his successors of the second, third, and fourth kingdoms, over the whole earth.

The denouement is seen in vision and interpretation in 2:34, 35 and 44, 45. "Thou sawest till that a stone was cut out without hands, which smote the image upon his feet that were of iron and clay, and brake them to pieces. Then was the iron, the clay, the brass, the silver, and the gold, broken to pieces together, and became like the chaff of the summer threshingfloors; and the wind carried them away, that no place was found for them: and the stone that smote the image became a great mountain, and filled the whole earth". "And in the days of these kings shall the God of heaven set up a kingdom, which shall never be destroyed: and the kingdom shall not be left to other people, but it shall break in pieces and consume all these kingdoms, and it shall stand for ever". Here then is the Bible specification for the basic meaning of one of its most characteristic concepts : this is the KINGDOM OF GOD: this is the KINGDOM OF HEAVEN.

Before proceeding to the parallel vision given to Daniel himself, and recorded in chapter 7, it will be well to pause here in chapter 2 and gather up some further important detail about the Kingdom of God. First, the Person in whom the Kingdom of God will be set up is without question identifiable; "the Stone cut out without hands". The instrument and its effect present a magnificent picture of Christ the King. In how many several settings is He called the Stone!

From the Mighty God of Jacob is promised "the Shepherd, the Stone of Israel" (Genesis 49:24). "The Stone which the builders refused is become the Headstone of the corner" (Psalm 118:22). "He shall be for...a Stone of stumbling and for a Rock of offence to both the houses of Israel" (Isaiah 8:14). "Behold, I lay in Zion for a foundation a Stone, a tried Stone, a precious corner Stone, a sure foundation" (Isaiah 28:16). Each of these passages, except the first, is quoted in the New Testament and the meaning is unquestionably Christ. In one epistle they are assembled, and a wealth of treasure made available for the Christian's heart. Here it is (1 Peter 2:4-8), as set out so illuminatingly in RV.

"Unto whom coming, a living Stone, rejected indeed of men, but with God elect, precious, ye also, as living stones, are built up a spiritual house, to be a holy priesthood, to offer up spiritual sacrifices, acceptable to God through Jesus Christ. Because it is contained in Scripture,

> *Behold, I lay in Zion a chief corner Stone, elect, precious:*
> *And he that believeth on him shall not be put to shame.*

For you therefore which believe is the preciousness: but for such as disbelieve,

> *The Stone which the builders rejected,*
> *The same was made the head of the corner;*

and,

> *A Stone of stumbling, and a Rock of offence."*

The Person in whom the Kingdom of God is to be set up is therefore Christ, but we also have this confirmed by a shaft of light unique to this one out of the many Scriptures which name Christ the Stone; "cut out without hands". The concept of representing a person's origin and parentage by his being cut out as a stone appears also in Isaiah 51:1 and 2: "look unto the rock whence ye are hewn...look unto Abraham your father and unto Sarah that bare you." In the light of this comment in Isaiah, there can be little doubt that "cut out without hands" is, in the language of Old Testament poetry, an indication that the Person in whom the Kingdom of God will be centred is a Person of no ordinary human lineage. Alongside so many other prophetic strains, we have here another indication that God's King will be of an origin outside this world and indeed owing nothing at all to the will of man. We must, then, put this word, "cut out without hands", alongside the name Immanuel, God with us, and "the Man that is Jehovah's fellow" (Zechariah 13:7), and respond, like Thomas bowing low at His feet, "My Lord and my God". Thus is surely to be fulfilled the divine decree, "Thou art my Son; this day have I begotten thee...I shall give thee the heathen for thine inheritance, and the uttermost parts of the earth for thy possession" (Psalm 2:7, 8); and "Let all the angels of God worship him".

This King, who is also our Saviour, is celebrated in His beauty and glory and majesty as King over all the earth by many another song of prophet and psalmist. The King "asked life of thee, and thou gavest it him, even length of days for ever and ever" (Psalm 21:4). "Unto us a child is born, unto us a son is given: and the government shall be upon his shoulder: and his name shall be called Wonderful, Counsellor, The mighty God, The everlasting Father, The Prince of Peace. Of the increase of his government and peace there shall be no end."

Next, this short passage sets in the clearest light the manner of the termination of these temporary kingdoms, and the substitution of the Kingdom of God which is not temporary: it shall never be destroyed nor left to other people, though it will be merged into the timeless rule of God. The Stone cut out without hands falls with violence on the fourth kingdom only, but the result is the utter destruction of the whole structure of Gentile rule over the earth. Daniel is thus explaining that though universal rule passes from the gold king to the silver king, and so on to the mixture of iron and clay, "those kings" continue to exist. When, however, the Kingdom of God is set up by this violent blow on the fourth kingdom, **all** the kings, the whole image, the whole structure of Gentile rule will be destroyed at once.

The prime characteristic of this picture is the sudden shattering of all previous rule and the substitution of a Kingdom in one sense the fifth member of a series, but in a more important sense a Kingdom entirely new. Perhaps the critical element here is best drawn out by reference to other Old Testament prophecies of the works of the Messiah. In nature a distant perspective minimises or even eliminates the apparent distance between objects seen afar. Two mountains may be ten miles apart – found indeed to be ten weary miles of "moor and fen, crag and torrent" if the traveller has to pass on foot from one to the other. But seen in the perspective of a distance of fifty miles, they may well appear to be equidistant. So it is with Old Testament prophecy. To this day the Jews, reading the Old Covenant with a veil on their hearts fail to distinguish the two comings of the Messiah. His coming was to be like "the waters of Shiloah that go softly" (Isaiah 8:6), and also a tempest of destruction. When He comes, "He shall not cry, nor lift up, nor cause his voice to be heard in the street. A bruised reed shall he not break, and the smoking flax shall he not quench" (Isaiah 42:2,3), but also He shall dash the nations in pieces like a potter's vessel (Psalm 2:9). In the very terms of this passage in Daniel, at His coming He would be both a Stone on whom many would fall in repentance and faith, and a Stone falling on men and grinding them to powder (Matthew 21:44).

There can be no question at all concerning which of these two manners of His coming is the one described by Daniel as the one establishing the Kingdom of God. In each of the couplets set out in the preceding paragraph, it is the second. His coming for this purpose is to be a sudden crashing destruction. To anticipate for a moment the imagery of Daniel chapter 7, as interpreted in Matthew 24:27, this coming, and this inauguration of the Kingdom will be like the lightning. There is nothing quiet, unseen, progressive, or gentle about it. After the first utter destruction, however, there is afterwards something progressive implied in the words, "the Stone...became a mountain, and filled the whole earth."

The **time** when the Kingdom of God will come is specified (so far as this single passage is concerned), in the words, "in the days of these kings" and that it is on the feet of the image, part of iron and part of clay, that the Stone fell. It is when the fourth kingdom has reached (in time) its final form that the destruction occurs. The period of unmixed iron (including the division into two parts), has passed completely. The period of feet (including ten toes, though not here mentioned), when the iron is mixed with clay, is also complete when the Kingdom of God will come. This part of our study, relating to the **time** of fulfilment, must be dealt with in a little more detail when we come to consider briefly chapter 7, but suffice to note at this moment that here is the point of the vision to which reference is made when Jesus began to preach the gospel of the Kingdom of God, and said, "The time is fulfilled".

At this point also, it is necessary to consider the question, Is it possible that in the intention of the Spirit of God this prophecy, the fifth kingdom, the kingdom of the Stone cut out without hands, can be fulfilled in the results of the preaching of the past 1,900 years, and in the existing church of Christ? The position taken in these pages is that even without regard to the vast mass of other parts of Scripture bearing on the subject, this is not really a debatable question. It is absolutely out of the question to take it so Augustine suggested an interpretation of the 1,000 years reign of Christ and binding of Satan in Revelation 20:1-6 which did away with the idea of a yet future earthly reign of Christ distinct from the church period. He wrote this as a tentative suggestion for reasons which anyone can read in the "City of God". Calvin followed his master on this point, and by way of the fugitives from the Marian persecutions (including John Knox) and their sojourn with Calvin, this view has never lost its hold in Britain and U.S.A. It is perpetuated in the traditional page headings often printed with the Authorized Version, and the Apostles' Creed is worded so as to leave room for it. Even if we take account only of Daniel's interpretation of Nebuchadnezzar's image, the nature of the "kingdoms" forming the subject from beginning to end, and the manner of establishment of the fifth kingdom, alone preclude completely the notion that the fifth Kingdom is the church of Christ.

Daniel's own vision of the kingdoms recorded in chapter 7, together with the interpretation furnished by "one of them that stood by", provide significant extensions and confirmation of what has been gleaned about the Kingdom of God from Nebuchadnezzar's vision. Although covering roug'ly the same ground and, like chapter 2 occurring in the portion of Daniel written in Chaldee, the differences are significant. The visions of chapter 7 and after, were given to Daniel personally and have a good deal to say about the saints and God's people.

The kingdoms of this later vision are seen by Daniel as wild and savage beasts, existing before, but held in check until the moment comes when each is allowed to take the kingdom and divide the earth. The beam of interest is overwhelmingly concentrated on the fourth beast and its successor, the Kingdom of the Son of Man and of the saints. We have the same kingdoms as in the image-vision but the fourth kingdom and the Kingdom of God occupy the visions from 7:7 to the end with the brief interlude of verse 17. What do we learn from this chapter about the Kingdom of God?

First, there is introduced for the first time a vision of God sitting on His throne and surrounded and served by myriad angelic beings. The ultimate disposal of the kingdom is in His hand. He is seen as an old, old, man (the Ancient of days) surrounded by all the means required for the instant execution of His will. In Nebuchadnezzar's image and its interpretation, the God of Heaven starts the course of Gentile dominion by giving unprecedented worldwide authority to Nebuchadnezzar. In Daniel's vision the Ancient of days terminates the course of Gentile dominion: "the beast was slain and his body destroyed and given to the burning flame" (verse 11).

In chapter 7:13, 14 the Kingdom called in chapter 2 God's Kingdom and heaven's Kingdom is given to the Son of Man, and it is on these subjects, the last kingdom as a ten-headed monster and the Son of Man coming with the clouds of heaven, that we reach the point where the New Testament both takes up the story and interprets the detail in an absolutely unmistakable manner.

In the later chapters of the Revelation, the last great world-power before the coming of Christ is pictured as a ten-horned beast. He appears first in Revelation 13:1 and several times in that chapter, and the next. In chapter 17 the scarlet beast with seven heads and ten horns is a principal actor in the scene. Eventually, now referred to simply as "the Beast", he assembles the kings and armies of the earth to fight against Christ: and so he comes to his end, "cast alive into a lake of fire burning with brimstone".

Few would doubt that the ten-horned beast of Daniel 7 and the Revelation are one and the same. Are they not both the final form of world power to be destroyed by Christ? Are there any signs in Revelation to identify this power? There are: chapter 17:9, "the seven heads are seven mountains on which the woman sitteth"; also chapter 17:18, "the woman thou sawest is that great city, which reigneth over the kings of the earth." In the reign of Vespasian, when these words were written (as stated in 17:10) there could not be the faintest doubt that these two descriptions — the seven hills and the great city which reigneth over the kings of the earth — signify Rome.

On this particular point, therefore, the light cast back on to Daniel 2 proves that the feet of the image on which the Stone fell is the Roman Empire, and this explains why in Mark 1:14, 15, it could be said "the time is fulfilled".

The next additional light is in Daniel 7:13, "and, behold, one like the Son of man came with the clouds of heaven". If Augustine was right, and it was at His first coming that Christ bound Satan and His saints reigned on thrones with Christ 1,000 years, then the Stone falling on the image and the Kingdom taken by the Son of man must have been at His first coming. Did Christ come at first with the clouds? The birth at Bethlehem was carolled by angels and revealed to shepherds, but there was no room for Him in the inn. There are in fact six or seven references in the New Testament to Christ's coming "with the clouds", and none could possibly doubt that they describe His **second** coming. The best known is, of course, Matthew 24:30, in a setting named as that of the prophet Daniel (verse 15), "They shall see the Son of man coming in the clouds of heaven with power and great glory". Thus, we have this additional light from Daniel 7:13 to confirm that the establishment of the Kingdom of God is to take place at the Second Advent of our Lord Jesus Christ.

Lastly, in Daniel 7 there is added the fact that when Christ comes to reign, His saints shall reign with Him. "Judgment was given to the saints of the Most High; and the time came that the saints possessed the Kingdom" (Daniel 7:22). "And the kingdom and dominion, and the greatness of the kingdom under the whole heaven, shall be given to the people of the saints of the Most High, whose kingdom is an everlasting kingdom, and all dominions shall serve and obey Him" (verse 27).

Without any attempt at a detailed exposition of the prophecy of Daniel, but confining attention to the few verses which are the root of all later Scriptures concerning the Kingdom of God, we shall see that every detail is of importance in searching the Scriptures of the New Testament in order to find, embrace, and practise all that will assist us in seeking first the Kingdom of God.

Chapter 5

SOME QUESTIONS ABOUT THE MILLENNIUM

Before continuing in detail with the real theme of these pages — the Kingdom of God between the first and second comings of Christ — one or two questions about the Millennium might be briefly considered. As everyone knows, the name Millennium arises from Revelation 20, where we read that after the Coming of Christ in the clouds of heaven, Satan will be bound, and deceive the nations no more for a thousand years. During this thousand years Christ will reign over the earth with His saints after the first resurrection. While there is some detail about this thousand years (a millennium) reign in the New Testament, most of the details we need to know about the glories and blessings of that perfect government of the world, are found in the Old Testament prophets. Certain evangelical Christians cannot escape from looking at the Millennium in terms of the currently developing social and political conditions, and in some subtle way such thoughts constitute an objection to the whole idea of an earthly reign of Christ. Such a Kingdom presents to their minds something unworthy to succeed the reign of love in a spiritual Kingdom now realised through the gospel. What (it has been demanded) kind of television programmes will be broadcast? How fast will aeroplanes fly? What will be the voting system? Probably such questions are not intended seriously, but rather intended to suggest objections to the Bible truth. Nevertheless they provide occasion to make clear some aspects of the Millennium not elsewhere considered in this book.

The first revulsion against Millennial teaching in the centuries before Augustine was itself a revulsion against mistaken expectations unrestrainedly indulged. A section of the Church manifested undue enthusiasm about the imagined delights of the Millennium — especially fleshly delights. There is an obvious parallel between the two points of view. If we imagine Christianity superficially accepted by a Muslim society or an American Indian society, and this acceptance were to be followed by a slipping back, then the former degenerates would naturally think of the Millennium in terms of the harem and the latter in terms of the "happy hunting-grounds". In our contemporary society the positions of the happy hunting-grounds tend to be occupied by the present state of evolution of scientific and political development. It is almost too obvious to point out that we must avoid reading into the Bible picture of a Millennium what might appear desirable or necessary to modern man.

The sample questions just quoted refer to conditions either highly transitory on any count (television and the speed of aeroplanes) or naked expedients for lack of better (democratic rule by the popular vote). Regarding communications, although by contrast with so little as two hundred years ago, television and the jet engine are stupendous marvels, they are in themselves but clumsy and bungling contrivances. The jet aero-engine is already overshadowed by space-flight. At the moment these words are being revised we hear that an unmanned Soviet spacecraft has made a soft landing on the planet Venus and the count-down has started for the third manned moon-landing. We may soberly expect that millennial communications will represent perfection, and not just some arbitrary stage in the development of human powers without God.

Still more inconceivably foolish it would be to imagine that the processes of democratic election will be involved in the perfect government promised for the millennial earth. Reflect on governmental failures in the field of disarmament, and compare Isaiah 2:3, 4. "Out of Zion shall go forth the law, and the word of the Lord from Jerusalem. And he shall judge among the nations, and shall rebuke many people: and they shall beat their swords into plowshares, and their spears into pruninghooks: nation shall not lift up sword against nation, neither shall they learn war any more". Let anyone go out and listen to and look at the electorate in any land. Will anyone soberly maintain that the person or the policy wanted by most people is best or wisest? The ballet box is a good thing because it permits change without a blood-bath, but very few can really believe that it chooses even the best men available, let alone the perfection of wisdom and power promised for the reign of Christ and the Kingdom of God. It is also necessary, if extremely sobering, to remember that there will not be continuity between the development of human society as we know it today and the Kingdom of God in the Millennium. If one thing is clear from the Scriptures of both the Old and New Testaments, it is that the judgments of God, destructive of man's world, will plough a deep furrow between what is now and what will be in that day.

That is not a just view of Scripture which regards the Kingdom of God in the Millennium as unworthy to succeed the reign of grace now realised in the Church through the preaching of the gospel. So far as the Church is concerned, what succeeds the present period of the Church militant is the Church glorified with Christ. "When that which is perfect is come, then that which is in part shall be done away...For now we see through a glass, darkly; but then face to face: now I know in part; but then shall I know even as also I am known". So far as the world is concerned, the Millennium will not be a descent from something higher to something lower (that is, from the spiritual reign of grace to the earthly reign of power), but nothing less than life from the dead.

It would be very unwise to attempt, on the basis of Scripture language, the detailed description of the social and political conditions of the Millennium, but the basic facts are everywhere so plain that we cannot fail to see them. Justice and peace are the two great characteristics, and it is just here that the human governments of the world have so conspicuously failed. The power and wisdom to maintain **both** justice and peace have been and are lacking in the best and wisest rulers. To maintain justice, peace has had to be abandoned; and in any case who has been wise enough to know unerringly where justice lies? In order to maintain peace, then justice has been found impossible. Pause for a moment, and reflect on the two verses quoted a few lines earlier from Isaiah 2:2, 3. Ask of yourself the question, in what conceivable sense they have ever for a moment been fulfilled during the gospel period, or are true today. Those words admit absolutely and indisputably of only two interpretations. They either promise a Millennium or they are false. No other possibility can for a moment be maintained. That there are difficulties and obscurities about the prophetic timetable, and about the interpretation of other Scriptures is not for a moment denied, but this passage from Isaiah 2, and many others like it, are so crystal clear and unambiguous, that even if we admit that we cannot fully explain other passages, the certain promise of a Millennial Kingdom of God must be a sheet anchor which it is impossible to hold in doubt. Admittedly, it is difficult, but by no means impossible, to understand why, in Acts 2:16-21 Peter applies to the gift of the Spirit at Pentecost, the prophecy of Joel 2:28-32 which the Old Testament context requires should be understood as ultimately fulfilled at the introduction of the Millennium. Equally clearly, the apostles elsewhere apply to the spread of the gospel to the Gentiles Scriptures which must ultimately apply to the blessing of the Gentiles in the Millennium. It may be true that Scripture light is not available to write beforehand the timetable of the 'end of the age' preceding the Millennium. In particular, if up to the Rapture of the saints all believers in Jesus, both Jew and Gentile, lose their distinctness in the Church, where does the believing Remnant of Jews come from? Where can time be found in the prophetic timetable for their conversion and commission? These are difficulties, and they may or may not come within the scope of what is revealed. But fifty difficulties must be held in abeyance in the presence of one word of God of indisputable meaning; and there is not only one passage of the class of Isaiah 2:3 and 4, but there are very many. In the interpretation of prophecy, the snare everywhere encountered is the temptation to believe that we possess the means of constructing a system including a complete understanding, with no gaps in knowledge. This has led many interpreters to ignore what is crystal clear, in order to construct a complete system. This is the point of view being here urged. If clear, certain, and unmistakable teaching is available, it must not be given up in order to force consistency with other passages. The interpretation of the other passages must, if necessary, be left in abeyance, for, as has already been quoted, "we know in part", and complete knowledge is not available to us yet. Such teaching, that is, of clear and indisputable meaning, is widely available in Scripture demanding belief in the Millennium.

"The government shall be upon his shoulder: and his name shall be called...The Prince of Peace. Of the increase of his government and peace there shall be no end, upon the throne of David, and upon his kingdom, to order it, and to establish it with judgment and with justice from henceforth even for ever." Under these banners, Justice and Peace, mankind will enjoy happiness and fulfilment without sin, freedom without violence. "He shall redeem their soul from deceit and violence...all nations shall call him blessed...and blessed be his glorious name for ever: and let the whole earth be filled with his glory; Amen, and Amen." (Psalm 72:14, 17, 19)

MATTHEW 5:1 - 20.

1 And seeing the multitudes, he went up into a mountain: and when he
2 was set, his disciples came unto him: And he opened his mouth, and
3 taught them, saying, Blessed are the poor in spirit : for theirs is the
4 kingdom of heaven. Blessed are they that mourn: for they shall be
5 comforted. Blessed are the meek: for they shall inherit the earth.
6 Blessed are they which do hunger and thirst after righteousness: for
7 they shall be filled. Blessed are the merciful: for they shall obtain
8,9 mercy. Blessed are the pure in heart: for they shall see God. Blessed are
10 the peacemakers: for they shall be called the children of God. Blessed
 are they which are persecuted for righteousness' sake: for theirs is the
11 kingdom of heaven. Blessed are ye, when men shall revile you, and
 persecute you, and shall say all manner of evil against you falsely, for
12 my sake. Rejoice, and be exceeding glad: for great is your reward in
13 heaven: for so persecuted they the prophets which were before you. Ye
 are the salt of the earth: but if the salt have lost his savour, wherewith
 shall it be salted? it is henceforth good for nothing, but to be cast out,
14 and to be trodden under foot of men. Ye are the light of the world. A
15 city that is set on an hill cannot be hid. Neither do men light a candle,
 and put it under a bushel, but on a candlestick; and it giveth light unto all
16 that are in the house. Let your light so shine before men, that they may
 see your good works, and glorify your Father which is in heaven.
17 Think not that I am come to destroy the law, or the prophets: I
18 am not come to destroy, but to fulfil. For verily I say unto you, Till
 heaven and earth pass, one jot or one tittle shall in no wise pass from
19 the law, till all be fulfilled. Whosoever therefore shall break one of these
 least commandments, and shall teach men so, he shall be called the least
 in the kingdom of heaven: but whosoever shall do and teach them, the
20 same shall be called great in the kingdom of heaven. For I say unto you,
 That except your righteousness shall exceed the righteousness of the
 scribes and Pharisees, ye shall in no case enter into the kingdom of
 heaven.

MATTHEW 5: 38 - 48.

38 Ye have heard that it hath been said, An eye for an eye, and a tooth for
39 a tooth; But I say unto you, That ye resist not evil: but whosoever shall
40 smite thee on thy right cheek, turn to him the other also. And if any
 man will sue thee at the law, and take away thy coat, let him have thy
41 cloak also. And whosoever shall compel thee to go a mile, go with him
42 twain. Give to him that asketh thee, and from him that would borrow
 of thee turn not thou away.
43 Ye have heard that it hath been said, Thou shalt love thy
44 neighbour, and hate thine enemy. But I say unto you, Love your
 enemies, bless them that curse you, do good to them that hate you, and

45 pray for them which despitefully use you, and persecute you; That ye may be the children of your Father which is in heaven: for he maketh his sun to rise on the evil and on the good, and sendeth rain on the just
46 and on the unjust. For if ye love them which love you, what reward
47 have ye? do not even the publicans the same? And if ye salute your brethren only, what do ye more than others? do not even the publicans
48 so? Be ye therefore perfect, even as your Father which is in heaven is perfect.

MATTHEW 7: 24 - 29.
24 Therefore whosoever heareth these sayings of mine, and doeth them, I
25 will liken him unto a wise man, which built his house upon a rock: And the rain descended, and the floods came, and the winds blew, and beat
26 upon that house; and it fell not: for it was founded upon a rock. And every one that heareth these sayings of mine and doeth them not, shall be likened unto a foolish man, which built his house upon the sand:
27 And the rain descended, and the floods came, and the winds blew, and
28 beat upon that house; and it fell: and great was the fall of it. And it came to pass, when Jesus had ended these sayings, the people were
29 astonished at his doctrine : For he taught them as one having authority, and not as the scribes.

Chapter 6

THE SERMON ON THE MOUNT

Of the three great Kingdom discourses of Christ in Matthew's Gospel, the first, in chapters 5 to 7, gives the laws controlling behaviour in the Kingdom, and the characters suitable to the Kingdom. "Seek ye first the kingdom of God," is a precept taken from Luke's form of this discourse, and if we seek to obey it we must give a high place to accepting the challenge of these chapters. Too often people adopt the defence mechanism of assuming that since this is a Kingdom and not a Church address, we can quietly ignore it for practical purposes. To read these chapters with conscience awake is to realise their challenge to everyone who names the name of Christ.

At this stage not a word is said to modify the expectation from Daniel's prophecy as to the form in which the Kingdom of God was to appear, except for several indications that these directions were to apply to disciples in a hostile world. It is first to be noted that the Great King here addresses Himself to confessed disciples. The way of salvation, of repentance and faith will not be found here, nor the redemptive work of Christ which makes them possible. The hearers are clearly understood to be disciples of the Master, and secure in the awareness of a settled relationship with their Father in heaven, and implied participation in His nature is the only hint of the power which produces such character and makes such behaviour possible.

As we have already remarked, it has been questioned whether these precepts are valid and mandatory for believers in the church dispensation. This suggestion must be examined, and it will easily be seen that there are senses in which the sermon shares the position of the Gospels generally, that of a transitional and intermediate period between what was proper to pious Jews as pictured, for example, in the opening chapters of Luke's Gospel, and the status of believers subsequent to the gift of the Holy Spirit. It would be foolish to ignore this transitional character. In John 16:12, 13 this incomplete nature of all that the Lord imparted to His disciples is made explicit: "I have yet many things to say unto you, but ye cannot bear them now. Howbeit, when he, the Spirit of truth, is come, he will guide you into all the truth." That this discourse presents a challenge greatly in advance on all that went before will emerge clearly in a moment; but the main point on which there remains something which falls short of the full New Testament position on the subject of Christian behaviour concerns the Law. This important question will be considered in greater detail later, but it will soon be seen that the terms in which the Law is here enforced and confirmed are not really out of harmony with Galatian truth, but most clearly leave room for it. When, positively, we see that the moral basis of this teaching is perfection, as God is perfect, (5:48) it must be recognised that we should abandon any reserve in applying these precepts to ourselves, and enter on a confrontation of conscience with precept, of set purpose, with boldness and courage, as well as with humility and contrition. Here is the beginning of seeking first the Kingdom of God. Here, first of all, is the point at which we will pour the first of our prayers, and the finest of our energies into the enterprise of seeking the Kingdom.

An analysis of the sayings collected together in these three chapters will serve to highlight their unity and completeness.

    I.   5: 1-16.   Disciples in a wicked world.
    II.   5:17-48.   The Kingdom's advance on the Law.
    III.   6: 1-18.   Good works: alms, prayer, fasting.
    IV.   6:19-34.   Material possessions.
    V.   7: 1-12.   Our brothers and our Father.
    VI.   7:13-27.   The true and the false.

I. vv. 3-12 contain the beatitudes, each one being introduced by the word 'blessed'. 'Blessed' is a characteristic Bible word, especially in the Psalms and in these paragraphs of the Gospels. It is to be clearly distinguished from the same English word in such usages as Ephesians 1:3 and 1 Peter 1:3 ("Blessed be the God and Father of our Lord Jesus Christ") or Matthew 21:9 ("Blessed is he that cometh in the name of the Lord"). In these latter cases it means something akin to 'praised' or 'worshipped'. In the beatitudes it is often said to be equivalent to 'happy'; but this needs qualification. Perhaps its meaning would be best represented by understanding that these are the people truly to be congratulated or even envied. In the Old English usage, (so long as we keep clear of any idea of a bow to the gods of chance!) these are the lucky people! In any society there exist the characters praised, cheered, congratulated, rewarded and envied by all their fellows. Indeed, to a very considerable extent the quality of a society is defined by the characters who receive its plaudits. Without question the adulation and material gain accorded to the idols of sport and entertainment are a most revealing exposure of the quality of our society and its values. Right in the forefront of what the Great King has to say about the Kingdom is the literally shocking list of its ideal characters: the poor, the mourners, the meek, thirsters after righteousness, merciful, pure, peaceable, persecuted. On earth these will inherit the Kingdom, and in heaven their reward is great.

In vv.13 to 16 the disciples are brought face to face with their responsibilities and privileges as the salt of the earth and the light of the world. It is by their witness that they fulfil these preservative and light-giving functions. There must be good works to be seen and witness to be heard. When men see their good works, then on hearing the witness they will glorify the Father of such people, whom they cannot see.

II. In this section, the relation between the law of Moses and the precepts of Christianity are explained. We shall find it important to weigh this matter from two points of view. One is the view taken by Jewish disciples looking forward, and the other takes account of the full light afforded in the Epistles and looks backward. We have to take account of the fact that the disciples then being addressed were Jews, and indeed that the whole of Matthew's Gospel is a vindication of Christianity addressed to Jews. The primary purpose of vv. 17 to 19 is to provide the disciples with an answer to charges such as issued in the accusation against Stephen, "We have heard him say that this Jesus of Nazareth shall destroy...the customs which Moses delivered us." Christ was not come to destroy the law, or the prophets. The true purpose of the law can never pass away. It must be fulfilled. There are at least two important ways in which this fulfilment is to be understood. First, in Jesus the types and sacrifices and prophecies of the law were fulfilled. Second, when believers would come to be in the full light and blessing of His work, then the righteousness of the law would be fulfilled in them. (Romans 8:3)

In vv.21 to 48 six examples are given which contrast the Old Testament law with the then present authoritative pronouncements of Christ. "It was said...but I say". These examples present the way whereby the law, not only as a means of justification, but also as a rule of life was to be annulled by being replaced by a rule of life which very much more than fulfils the law. At the same time the law continues unimpaired as God's standard for condemnation, but never giving life. In this way we can see how vv.17 to 19 leaves room for the fullest light for the Christian in Galatians. At the same time vv.21 to 48 are already, and explicitly, so great an advance on the law that nothing can be higher than the standard of these six examples, for they end "Be ye perfect, as your heavenly Father is perfect." No standard could be higher than this, and no standard for the disciple should be lower.

In each case the restraint of the new code searches not only the act, (murder v.21, adultery v.27, divorce v.31, oaths v.35, revenge v.38, enmity v.43) as did the law of Moses, but also the state of mind, heart and spirit from which the action springs — a vast step! Each of these issues is as alive and pressing today as it ever was, and their condemnation of the standards of a permissive society as devastating. To be a Christian is to be a fearless rejector of the morals of every permissive society, from that of Corinth to that of the late twentieth century. This is not to deprive the Christian of the good life, but to guide him on the road to the highest good. In the end it will appear that the Christian's natural power of will is not pitted against the seductions of all permissive societies, but he is given a new power from God. This part of the truth will follow later, but in this place, and by this voice, the standards are unequivocally proclaimed, and we must proclaim them with the same stark clarity, yet with humility. The last two of the six, relating to revenge and hatred, will serve as examples showing how the principles are to be worked out in detail. The English philosopher Hobbes in his "Leviathan" presented the concept of the state of mere nature, and his celebrated dictum was that in this state human life is "nasty, brutish, and short". It is against this kind of background that we are to see the restraint on the "state of nature" imposed by the law of Moses. A man in this state of nature who suffered damage to his eye would never consider inflicting exactly equivalent damage on his assailant. He would go beyond. His state of mind is exactly presented in the case of Lamech in Genesis 4:23, who boasted in a chant to his wives. "I have slain a man for wounding me!" It might be sufficient for Cain to avenge himself sevenfold, but Lamech would demand seventy-seven.

To this spirit and behaviour the law of Moses brought restraint, the restraint of strict justice. Revenge must be exactly equivalent to the injury, for an eye, an eye, and no more: for a tooth, a tooth, and no more. Shylock had to admit the impossibility of this in practice, but the principle of restraint on the tempestuous passions of man to strict justice is clear in the law of Moses. How immeasurable a step forward, and how unattainable a standard in merely human strength, appears in this new morality now proclaimed by Jesus. "But I say unto you, Love your enemies." It is not any longer to be a question of restraining the extent to which your hatred of your enemy may be expressed, but hatred, motivating revenge, is to be replaced by love, blessing, doing good, and prayer. How many apparently insoluble personal problems would be solved by simply obeying v.44: "Bless them that curse you,...pray for them which despitefully use you."

vv.45 to 48 then point the way to God's action to make the impossible possible, and that is to make men His children. v.45 is perhaps the greatest of the sayings called by Chesterton 'gigantesque'. God's goodness is as absolutely impartial as the sun and the rain, and it is in this sense that the disciples were to imitate their Father's perfection.

Taking on the other hand the backward look from the complete revelation given in the epistles, we find that the idea that the law of Moses is to be the rule of life for the Christian has such formidable backing, that we shall find it worth while to go over again in a little more detail the case for rejecting this view decisively. The verse from Matthew 5 most convincingly pressed into service to maintain the law as the Christian's rule of life is v.19. "whosoever shall do and teach (these commandments) shall be called great in the kingdom of heaven." Our method of proceeding to a true understanding of this teaching will be to recognise and reflect on the significance of two unquestionable facts − the transitional nature of the Gospels, and the teaching of the two foundation New Testament epistles, Galatians and Romans, and then in the light of these, to examine the passage itself more minutely. John 16:12-25 has already been quoted to show beyond all possible question that all teaching in the Gospels is transitional. Let this fact be duly weighed.

A little more space must be devoted to the fully-developed New Testament position concerning the Law, not enough to display the matter in full detail, but sufficient to guide a sincere student in his search. The pertinent passages are, in Galatians, the whole essential purpose and argument of the epistle, and in Romans, 7:1 to 8:4. This is not a side issue for Christian living, but one on which Paul makes his most emphatic and indeed intolerant affirmations. "Though...an angel from heaven preach any other gospel unto you than that which I have preached unto you, let him be accursed." Let all law-teachers ponder this terrific invective and examine his manner of teaching the commandments. The writer's subject in Galatians is the means of justification in God's sight, but also "the life that I now live in the flesh" (Galatians 2:20), that is, the means of perfecting Christian living after a true beginning by faith and not works, by the Spirit and not by the law (Galatians 3:2, 3). There would be general agreement amongst evangelicals on the former, the means of justification, but a profound cleavage on the latter, which is our present subject, as well as that of Galatians. The instruction of Galatians and Romans can be summarised as follows. Before the coming and sacrifice of Christ, God's people were individually in the **child** condition, differing nothing from servants, and under a tutor, the law, by which they were bound, and under which they were in bondage. Since the coming and sacrifice of Christ and the gift of the Spirit, God's people are all **sons** of God by faith; they are free, and no longer bound by the Law. In place of the Law as the rule of life for the Christian, is the Spirit. In consequence, the life now lived by the Christian in the body, if he walks in the Spirit (Galatians 5:16) and after the Spirit (Romans 8:4) is superior to anything the Law could produce, but nevertheless fulfils it. The manifestations of such a life are higher than anything the Law ever produced, but do not transgress it. "Against such there is no law" (Galatians 5:23). "The righteousness of the law is fulfilled." (Romans 8:4) A reversion to making the Law the rule of life is a fall, that is, something inferior (Galatians 5:4). This teaching is also vividly clear on the honour due to the Law and the true purpose of it. It is spiritual, holy, just and good, but it can only produce condemnation and death; by it sin becomes exceeding sinful (Romans 7:5-14). It was our schoolmaster or tutor to bring us to Christ, and "after that faith is come, we are no longer under a schoolmaster." (Galatians 3:24, 25)

And now we can examine the transitional teaching of Matthew 5:19 in the full New Testament light. We shall not truly honour our Lord's words here by making them contradict the teaching He gave after the coming of the Spirit. In 5:17 and 18 the subject is the fulfilment of the law and the prophets. "Think not that I am come to destroy the law, or the prophets: I am not come to destroy, but to fulfil. For verily I say unto you, Till heaven and earth pass, one jot or one tittle shall in no wise pass from the law, till all be fulfilled." This is in no way out of harmony with Galatian teaching, but, as has been mentioned earlier, has probably a rather more positive meaning in its own right than the ethical. "Till all be fulfilled" seems to indicate also that the law and the prophets foretold events which will all be fulfilled. The typical meaning of certain parts of the Law, the sacrifices, for example, were yet, at the time, to appear. The feasts of Jehovah probably have meaning alongside the prophets which reach still into the future for their fulfilment. In v.19, "whosoever shall do and teach them" is in antithesis with what precedes, "whosoever shall break one of these least commandments, and shall teach men so, shall be called least in the kingdom of heaven." The most rigorous adherence to the law-teaching of Romans and Galatians would not lead a person to break the commandments or to teach men to break them. Rather it would lead us to adopt a higher principle of living than the legal, and this principle would nevertheless fulfil the Law. Did Paul "do and teach" the commandments? Of course he did. His epistles are law-teaching and law-fulfilling in a sense much higher than that of the Pharisees. For I believe we must give the most favourable interpretation to the phrase "righteousness of the scribes and Pharisees" in v.20. Perhaps we could paraphrase the word 'righteousness' in this verse as 'living in accordance with God's requirement'. The fact that in the succeeding six examples the Lord quotes verbatim precepts from the Old Testament for correction by 'but I say unto you', shows the meaning He had in mind in talking of the righteousness of the scribes and Pharisees. The latter expression means exactly 'living under the law of commandments as the rule of life'. And the disciples were here most explicitly being taught to look for and embrace a rule of living which exceeds living by the law. This appears both in the occurrence of the word 'exceed' in v.20 and in the examples of what exceeds the law-teaching in vv.21, 27, 31, 38, and 43. The disciples were thus plainly prepared for the coming of a rule of life higher than either the Law or law in general. Every scribe instructed into the Kingdom of heaven will know and understand, will teach and do, in accordance with the Master's teaching as completed by the promised Spirit's teaching in the epistles.

The remaining sections III to VI of the Sermon on the Mount will not here be dealt with in detail. Either they work out in other examples the warning against mere externalism in religion, or they deal with subjects which have already been considered in our first chapter. In 7:1 the final precept, leading to the parable of the houses built on the sand or rock, is to contrast **saying** Lord, Lord," and **doing** the will of our Father in heaven. In Kingdom truth, and to this we shall have to return more than once, hearing and confessing are very important indeed: but hearing and saying are by themselves not enough. The acid test is action: to hear these sayings and to do them.

MATTHEW 13:10 to 17

10 And the disciples came, and said unto him, Why speakest thou unto
11 them in parables? He answered and said unto them, Because it is given unto you to know the mysteries of the kingdom of heaven, but to them
12 it is not given. For whosoever hath, to him shall be given, and he shall have more abundance: but whosoever hath not, from him shall be taken
13 away even that he hath. Therefore speak I to them in parables: because they seeing see not; and hearing they hear not, neither do they
14 understand. And in them is fulfilled the prophecy of Esaias, which saith, By hearing ye shall hear, and shall not understand; and seeing ye
15 shall see, and shall not perceive: For this people's heart is waxed gross, and their ears are dull of hearing, and their eyes they have closed; lest at any time they should see with their eyes and hear with their ears, and should understand with their heart, and should be converted, and I
16 should heal them. But blessed are your eyes, for they see: and your
17 ears, for they hear. For verily I say unto you, That many prophets and righteous men have desired to see those things which ye see, and have not seen them; and to hear those things which ye hear, and have not heard them.

Chapter 7

THE MYSTERIES OF THE KINGDOM

The seven parables of the thirteenth chapter of Matthew's Gospel make up the second great Kingdom discourse. After listening with the crowd to the parable of the sower, the disciples came to the Lord apart and asked Him why He was teaching by parables. "He answered and said unto them, Because it is given unto you to know the mysteries of the Kingdom of heaven, but to them it is not given." (verse 11) In this verse is a critical advance in the progress of the revelation of Kingdom truth, and although the subject has been introduced in an earlier chapter, the most careful consideration must now be devoted to it.

In the chapters intervening between seven and thirteen there are four references to the Kingdom, and it is a matter of some interest that in two of these the expression used is not 'the Kingdom of heaven', but the 'Kingdom of God' or simply 'the Kingdom'. These references will not be given special attention at this moment, beyond noting that they might well have sounded mysterious to those who heard them before the explanation now given. In His commendation of the centurion's faith, the Lord said to the crowds who were following Him, "Many shall come from the east and west, and shall sit down with Abraham, and Isaac, and Jacob, in the Kingdom of heaven". (8:11) A little later the Pharisees committed the unpardonable sin of attributing the liberation of the demoniac to Beelzebub. In reply, the Lord vigorously repudiates this charge, and explains that the intervention of God in power for the liberation of man from devils is the Kingdom of God. "If I cast out devils by the Spirit of God, then the Kingdom of God is come unto you". In these two sayings, uttered in the hearing of the crowds, the Lord would appear to them, and indeed was, witnessing both to the fact of a Kingdom then present, and at the same time to a Kingdom promised for the future when all the saints of all ages would enter into their fulfilment and reward. How could both be true? The new revelation now to be given explains this riddle for the first time.

These references and the chapters in which they occur also bear witness to the state of affairs which made this the opportune moment for the new revelation. The picture presented is of the national leaders with eyes wide open withholding acceptance of the Kingdom being preached, and recognition of and submission to the Person in whom that Kingdom had come near. In superlative degree the Lord Jesus had shown Himself to possess every quality required to fit Him for the throne. See His compassion in 9: 36. "When he saw the multitudes, he was moved with compassion on them, because they fainted, and were scattered abroad, as sheep having no shepherd". Being moved with compassion, would His wisdom be equal to guiding the people aright? Behold in the Sermon on the Mount the laws forming a Kingdom which would indeed be the desire of all nations, the guidelines for a society promoting man's highest good. Given the compassion and the wisdom, would He wield the power to deliver men from the Evil One? Those who are most familiar with the story are as much as any in danger of overlooking the stupendous marvel of His instant mastery over all the foes of mankind, from those which have by the development of the highest human powers been with difficulty kept in check, to those which have without a single exception defeated the efforts of the greatest. In the portion of the story contained within the limits of only two chapters, Matthew eight and nine, disease, demons, tempest, and even death itsèlf are under His control. Where He rules, these foes will not any longer remain to bring suffering and sorrow. Gather together the wisdom of all the philosophers and the knowledge of all science and the might of every conqueror and it will be found that a start has scarcely been made to master these four tormentors of man. Jesus was master of all, and yet He was "despised and rejected of men; a man of sorrows, and acquainted with grief: and we hid as it were our faces from him; he was despised, and we esteemed him not". In the wisdom and knowledge of God, the full proof of man's evil, as well as the full power of God's love, required such a climax as the rejection and crucifixion of Jesus, and so there was necessary a form of the Kingdom of God suitable to a King refused and therefore absent in heaven.

Attention must first be given to seizing the full import of the words 'mystery' and 'mysteries' as everywhere understood in bible times. The word 'secret' in A.V. of Daniel 2 represents the meaning of Nebuchadnezzar's dream, and the LXX translation of the same word is **'musterion'**. In the Greek language from the earliest times and right through the bible period the word 'mystery' meant a secret, the knowledge of which was greatly to be desired by men and imparted special powers and privileges to men who possessed it. Such knowledge was unattainable by human powers, and was capable of reception only by the initiated. Great importance was attached to the process of initiation, and thereafter such knowledge could only be imparted to men by God, revealing it by His Spirit. This word evidently served the purpose of the Spirit of God, since it is taken over by the inspired writers of Holy Scripture, and a Christian meaning given at every point.

The passage now under consideration is the first example of the New Testament mysteries, and like several others, has special reference to the period between the first and second comings of Christ, a period relatively unilluminated by Old Testament prophecy. A distinguishing feature of this first New Testament mystery is that in two out of the three Gospels where it occurs, the plural 'mysteries' is used. In non-biblical literature the plural 'mysteries' described the rites of the mystery-religions. I can only suggest that in Matthew and Mark the plural 'mysteries' denotes each of the parables of Matthew thirteen as separately a mystery, and perhaps our study of them will confirm the justness of this view.

By the Lord's use of the word mystery, therefore, we are prepared to expect the divine revelation of a secret hitherto hidden. Every part of the expectation aroused by the introduction of this word is satisfied in the verses 11 to 17 which form the general part of the Lord's answer to the disciples' question, Why speakest Thou unto them in parables? Is this secret worth knowing? Is it greatly desirable? Read verses 16 and 17. "Blessed are your eyes, for they see: and your ears, for they hear. For verily I say unto you, That many prophets and righteous men have desired to see those things which ye see, and have not seen them; and to hear those things which ye hear, and have not heard them." Is its reception greatly dependent on the spiritual history and condition of the hearers? Indeed it is. The crowds and the leaders could not see or hear rightly because their heart was waxed gross, and their ears dull of hearing, and their eyes they had themselves closed. The disciples could see and hear because they were disciples. They had accepted the authority and the Person of the Divine King Himself, and it was by His revealing authority that they could hear and understand.

In what sense was the Kingdom of heaven and the Kingdom of God a secret hitherto hidden? It was no secret that the Kingdom would certainly come. In our chapters three and four we have already remarked on this and described in some detail the Kingdom as Daniel foresaw it. What Daniel prophesied the wise understood. The secret hitherto unrevealed was the **form** in which the Kingdom would at first be seen. No contrast could be greater than that between events which inaugurate the two forms of the Kingdom. The Kingdom as foreseen by Daniel begins with the coming of Christ like the lightning, which every eye shall see. The LORD shall send the rod of His strength out of Zion. He shall rule in the midst of His enemies. His people shall be willing in the day of His power. The Kingdom in its mysteries was to be inaugurated by the Sower going forth to sow the seed of the Word of God, in the manner we shall shortly study in detail. The seven mysteries of the Kingdom of heaven begin with the personal activity of Christ here in Person in the world, the story of which activity unfolds itself in Matthew as we have seen. "He that soweth the good seed is the Son of Man". And they end with the harvest at the end of the age. In Matthew we learn that the end of the age is the period immediately preceding the coming of Christ in the clouds of heaven. They thus unfold the story of the Kingdom over the whole period between the first and the second comings. During the Kingdom when established in power in the future, Satan will be bound and shut up, "that he should deceive the nations no more, till the thousand years should be fulfilled". During all the period of the Kingdom mysteries, the enemy will be most active in his efforts to nullify and to frustrate the effects of the Word in spreading the Kingdom.

It is our purpose to examine the seven mysteries in some detail, but it will be useful to make some general observations at this stage. The parables of Matthew thirteen are naturally divided into two classes, by the fact that the first four were uttered in the hearing of the multitudes by the sea side, while the last three were given to the disciples alone, inside the house. "Then Jesus sent the multitude away, and went into the house: and his disciples came unto him." (13: 36) Three parables were explicitly interpreted by the Lord, and apparently all the explanations were spoken to the disciples alone. While it is plain that the crowds did not understand even what they heard, yet the first four parables present the mystery Kingdom in its outward form as seen by the sea of the nations, while the last three present an inside view, as the heart of God is engaged in it. In the latter, there is no active energy of evil.

Within this broad distinction, we may distinguish two pairs in the·first group of four parables. The first two parables, both concerned with sowing the seed, cover the whole period from one point of view, and bring us already to the end of the age. The third and fourth parables, those of the mustard seed and the leaven, present particular views of the ways in which the mature system is permeated with evil. The last three dwell on the joy of the King in what gleams and glows through all the evil, the treasure and the pearl, and, in the last, the care taken to garner "the good". In the treasure and the pearl we come to the point where the two great themes of the Church and the Cross enter into the Kingdom mysteries.

"Therefore every scribe which is instructed unto the kingdom of heaven is like unto a man that is an householder, which bringeth forth out of his treasure things new and old." (verse 52) Here is an objective for all who seek first the Kingdom — to be well-supplied householders who can make good provision for household or for guests. Perhaps the idea of a scribe instructed unto the Kingdom envisages a scribe in whose mind and heart are stored the treasures of the Old Testament. If such a man were to become a disciple, he would then add immeasurably to his treasure, by becoming instructed unto the Kingdom. Let every reader list high amongst the aims on which he expends the best of his energies, to be such a scribe, to be such a householder, and, under the Master, to be able to dispense such a treasure.

MATTHEW 13:3 to 9 and 18 to 23

3 And he spake many things unto them in parables, saying, Behold, a
4 sower went forth to sow; And when he sowed, some seeds fell by the
5 way side, and the fowls came and devoured them up: Some fell upon stony places, where they had not much earth: and forthwith they
6 sprung up, because they had no deepness of earth: And when the sun was up, they were scorched; and because they had no root, they
7 withered away. And some fell among thorns; and the thorns sprung up,
8 and choked them: But other fell into good ground, and brought forth
9 fruit, some an hundredfold, some sixtyfold, some thirtyfold. Who hath ears to hear, let him hear.
18 Hear ye therefore the parable of the sower.
19 When anyone heareth the word of the kingdom, and understandeth it not, then cometh the wicked one, and catcheth away that which was
20 sown in his heart. This is he which received seed by the way side. But he that received the seed into stony places, the same is he that heareth
21 the word, and anon with joy receiveth it; Yet hath he not root in himself, but dureth for a while: for when tribulation or persecution
22 ariseth because of the word, by and by he is offended. He also that received seed among the thorns is he that heareth the word; and the care of this world, and the deceitfulness of riches, choke the word, and
23 he becometh unfruitful. But he that received seed into the good ground is he that heareth the word, and understandeth it: which also beareth fruit, and bringeth forth, some an hundredfold, some sixty, some thirty.

Chapter 8

THE PARABLE OF THE SOWER

On a certain now famous day in the later part of the sixteenth century, some kind of service was proceeding in the Cathedral at Pisa, and whether by homily, Missal or Breviary, the Word of God was being proclaimed. But this, one of the greatest influences ever invading the world, was quite lost on one person present. The young Galileo was otherwise engaged. Present in body, his mind was intently and eagerly occupied with a huge bronze lamp slung from the vaulted ceiling. Like many another before and since, he saw that it was slowly swinging, but unlike them, he was making this observation the subject of measurement as exact as the means immediately at his disposal permitted. He used his pulse to time the oscillations, and came to the most unexpected conclusion that the number of swings per minute was independent of the length of the swing, and was indeed constant for that particular lamp. It was one of the conspicuous moments in the history of scientific discovery, and this fact rather intensifies than diminishes the impact of the story as an illustration of the meaning of the parable of the sower. The Lord gives in a sentence the precept, for the hearer, to which the parable leads: "Take heed therefore how ye hear". (Luke 8:18) When the Word of God is preached, many are the enemies resisting its effect on the hearer; let nothing, however important in itself, interfere with your hearing the Word.

The paramount lesson of the parable is that the appointed instrument of increasing the Kingdom in its present form is the preaching of the Word of God. The effect of the Word in individual cases is limited and constrained by hostile influences, as well as by the preparedness of the hearer, but the Word contains in itself all the power needed to effect what God desires. This truth can be illustrated in detail from the Acts, where the Word is often almost personified as the agent achieving results for God as it works in the world. No lesson can be of greater importance than this for "seeking first the Kingdom," whether we consider what can effect the changes so much needed in ourselves, or the means by which we can be of service to God in affecting others. "Study to show thyself approved unto God, a workman that needeth not to be ashamed, rightly dividing the word of truth," (2 Timothy 2:15)

The general lines of interpretation are clear and indeed are supplied by the Lord to the disciples apart. The seed is the Word, the Word of the

Kingdom, or the Word of God. The sower is not named in the explanation of the first parable, and from this we may conclude that although the Son of Man is at first the Sower, as in the parable of the tares, all who preach the Word before the second coming of Christ will be sharing in the work of sowing. The ground on which the seed falls represents the hearts of those who hear, but we should be quite clear that this includes all who hear the Word of God, and not only the unconverted. In at least one of the four examples described, the plant springing from the seed shows life and then dies. (Matthew 13: 5) This fact should surely lead us to think, not so much of those who receive the Saviour and thereby pass once and for all from death unto life, but of those who do in fact obey Christ for a time — (that is, form part of His Kingdom) — and then cease to do so. It is only too sadly true to experience to see people living as Christians for a time, and then falling away. The fruit, when it appears, is not only the salvation of the soul received, although this is always involved, but lives lived under the authority of the Lord. The fruit is the Kingdom of God, the authority of Christ, deepened and spread.

The practical consequences of this distinction are very great. If we read the parable with the assumption that a successful result means primarily a soul saved from death and judgment, then once our own calling and election are sure, we can, so to speak with a little exaggeration, fold our arms on this point, and think only of the salvation of others. The truth is that we only rightly read this parable when we are alive to the fact that the enemies named are active to sap away our acceptance of the authority of Christ today, and tomorrow, and every time we hear the Word of God. It is not less true in the subjective sense, that the fruit is "righteousness, peace and joy in the Holy Ghost". Every Christian reader should therefore read the parable with watchfulness on two fronts. On the one hand we should be careful to learn about the use of the Word as the instrument for spreading the Kingdom. On the other hand we should take heed how we hear, since we are also the subjects in that Kingdom. The spread of the Kingdom relative to myself is the deepening establishment of the authority of Christ in my life. This means that I obey Him more simply and fully. In an ideal situation, when a child obeys its parents, such obedience is the child's link with the parents' mature experience and knowledge and the plans which flow from these. When the disciple obeys Christ in the details of life, then this obedience links the disciple's actions with all the breadth and length and depth and height of all that is in the heart of God and to which He is working. Surely this is the reason for the prominence given to the Kingdom of God from beginning to end of the New Testament.

Permeating the whole parable and the interpretation is the idea of conflict. The seed is immediately and always working and urging towards the production of fruit, but enemies are ceaselessly active and directed towards bringing to nothing the inherent fruit-producing power in the seed. Every time and by whatever means we are exposed to the influence of God's Word, the parable of the sower is re-enacted. The enemies are busy, and they are here identified so that we might be warned and prepared and pray against them.

Here is the first example contained in the parable, together with the interpretation. "And when he sowed, some seeds fell by the way side, and the fowls came and devoured them up." "When anyone heareth the word of the kingdom, and understandeth it not, then cometh the wicked one, and catcheth away that which was sown in his heart. This is he which received seed by the way side." (Matthew 13: 4, 19) In this case the heart is trodden by the everyday concerns of living. Whether these concerns are elevated or degraded is totally irrelevant in this context. Whatever may be their quality they render the heart impervious to the seed: it lies on the surface, and never makes any kind of entrance. One example is quoted in Luke's account. "Those by the way side are they that hear; then cometh the devil, and taketh away the word out of their hearts, lest they should believe and be saved." (Luke 8:12) The story of Galileo and the discovery of the principle of the pendulum is á perfect illustration of such a case. But which Christian does not recognise himself at times in this picture of the good seed of the Word of God falling by the way side? In every such case, it is desolating to reflect that this particular fragment of seed does nothing towards effecting its quota of Kingdom fruit, of fostering obedience to Christ, and hence of righteousness, joy and peace. How often must we all confess, "alas! what weakness within myself I find: no infant's changing pleasure is like my wandering mind."

The enemy is in this case most distinctly identified: the wicked one, Matthew 13: 19; Satan, Mark 4: 15; the devil, Luke 8: 12. If every hearer is oblivious, this enemy is awake to the immensity of the issues at stake when anyone is exposed to the action of the Word, and is ever ready to catch away the seed from the trodden heart.

In case two, the defect is shallowness, and the enemies are tribulation or persecution, (Matthew); afflication or persecution, (Mark); temptation or trial, (Luke), represented by the scorching power of the sun. Evidently in this case the story is taken a little forward from the time of immediate hearing of the Word. There is time for a period of enthusiastic response. But soon the enemies do their work and it all comes to nothing. It is important to recognise that the enemies are not in this case the critical factor, since they include much that is the common lot of man. "There hath no temptation taken you but such as is common to man: but God is faithful, who will not suffer you to be tempted above that ye are able; but will with the temptation also make a way to escape, that ye may be able to bear it." Nevertheless we are here warned that these experiences are potentially capable of reducing to nothing the effect of the Word, if we are not prepared against them.

Affliction is indeed often permitted by God to come upon His children for their good, and this recollection stresses the main lesson of this section of the parable, that shallowness, lack of root in ourselves, is the real cause of the withering. "It is true that the light and warmth of the sun are more often used to set forth the genial and comfortable workings of God's grace; but not always. As that heat, had the plant been rooted deeply enough, would have furthered its growth, and hastened its ripening, fitting it for the sickle and the barn — so these tribulations would have furthered the growth in grace of the true Christian, and ripened him for heaven. But as the heat scorches the blade which has no deepness of earth, and has sprung up on a shallow ground, so the troubles and afflictions which would have strengthened a true faith, cause a faith which was merely temporary to fail. When these afflictions for the truth's sake arrive, 'he is offended,' as though some strange thing had happened to him: for then are the times of sifting and of winnowing; and then, too, everyone that has no root, or, as Matthew describes it, 'no root in himself,' no inward root, withers away...As the roots of a tree are out of sight, while yet from them it derives its firmness and stability, so upon the hidden life of the Christian, that life which is out of sight of other men, his firmness and stability depend;...Compare 2 Corinthians 4: 17, 18, where faith in the unseen eternal things is the root, which, as Paul declares, enables him to count the present affliction light, and to endure to the end. Demas, on the other hand, lacked that root...Paul's condition at Rome at the moment when Demas forsook him was one of extreme outward trial and danger. It would seem probable, then, that the immediate cause of his going back was the tribulation which came for the Word's sake." (R.C. Trench)

In case three some seed "fell among thorns; and the thorns sprung up and choked them." "He also that received seed among the thorns is he that heareth the word; and the care of this world, and the deceitfulness of riches, choke the word, and he becometh unfruitful." (Matthew 13: 7, 22) "And the cares of this world, and the deceitfulness of riches, and the lusts of other things entering in, choke the word, and it becometh unfruitful." (Mark 4: 19) Yet again in Luke, "when they have heard, go forth, and are choked with cares and riches and pleasures of this life, and bring no fruit to perfection." (Luke 8: 14) The new group of enemies now introduced are even more evidently long-term and insidious in their action. In other contexts these three might never be joined together, but here they stand unmasked as the foes which, after the Word has been heard, and the hearer has "gone forth," choke it. They are likened to assailants who silently take hold; secure the hold against the victim's struggles; and slowly but surely bring resistance to an end in death.

Care, in the strict sense of anxiety or worry, has already come under the spotlight in an earlier chapter as something to be excluded altogether from the life of the disciple. In that place, we surveyed some of the warnings against worry spread so widely in Scripture, together with helps to overcome it. The role assigned to anxiety in this parable of the sower is even more positive and sinister than in the passages there considered. It is found in evil company as one of the influences which, if not vigorously dealt with at an early stage, will surely bring fruitfulness in the Kingdom to an end. It is never out of place to repeat the antidotes: faith, child-like yet mighty, in our Father's care: prayer, bringing the peace of God to garrison our hearts: positive action, seeking first the Kingdom.

Riches are not in themselves marked as evil or inconsistent with fruitfulness. Right back to Joseph of Arimathaea, a rich man, but also good and just and one who waited for the Kingdom of God, there has followed a noble succession of the few men of wealth who yet sought first the Kingdom. The warnings are against the **love** of money and the **deceitfulness** of riches. In this place it is surely the false appearance that riches so often present that bears the emphasis. The will to be rich does not reside in all. Indolence is in many cases stronger. But the urge to lay up treasure for oneself, where it exists, is responsible for so many resounding casualties, because it is so specious and plausible. In many things we all fail, but we must not fail for lack of the clear statement that the will to be rich is to be utterly excluded as motive or aim so far as the disciple is concerned. In its place the disciple acts on this: "and whatsoever ye do, do it heartily, as to the Lord, and not unto men; knowing that of the Lord ye shall receive the reward of the inheritance." (Colossians 3:23, 24) Let us simply hear the Word of God on this theme, in addition to the admonition concerning covetousness in Luke 12. "Ye cannot serve God and mammon (riches)." (Luke 16:13) "They that will be rich fall into temptation and a snare, and into many foolish and hurtful lusts, which drown men in destruction and perdition. For the love of money is a root of all evil: which while some coveted after, they have erred from the faith, and pierced themselves through with many sorrows...Charge them that are rich in this world, that they be not high-minded, nor trust in uncertain riches, but in the living God, who giveth us richly all things to enjoy; that they do good, that they be rich in good works, ready to distribute, willing to communicate; laying up in store for themselves a good foundation against the time to come, that they may lay hold on eternal life." (1 Timothy 6: 9, 10, 17-19)

Pleasure has always assumed an immense importance in human life, not only because, and at the level, that the natural man always seeks pleasure (and at this level we are alive in one of the distinctly pleasure-loving societies,) but because from the earliest times there have been serious thinkers who have been hedonists, that is they have equated the Good with pleasure. One of the most widely known of these, for the reason that he is mentioned in the Bible, (Acts 17:18) is Epicurus. This is not a place to enter on an attempt at a critique of the philosophy of Hedonism, but to see with what plainness Scripture in all its parts forbids the disciple's permitting earthly pleasure as a motive or aim. There are many things which will rightly give him pleasure, but pleasures pursued for their own sake are among the enemy's hands choking the good seed. The Greek word from which the hedonistic philosophy took its name occurs in Scripture in the following passages in addition to Luke 8: 14 which is at the moment under consideration. "For we ourselves also were sometimes foolish, disobedient, deceived, serving divers lusts and pleasures, living in malice and envy, hateful, and hating one another." (Titus 3: 3) "From whence come wars and fightings among you? Come they not hence, even of your pleasures that war in your members? Ye ask, and receive not, because ye ask amiss, that ye may consume it upon your pleasures." (James 4: 1-3) "This know also, that in the last days perilous times shall come. For men shall be...lovers of pleasures more than lovers of God." (2 Timothy 3:4) No reader of the English Bible could forget two related passages. "By faith Moses, when he was come to years, refused to be called the son of Pharaoh's daughter; choosing rather to suffer affliction with the people of God, than to enjoy the pleasures of sin for a season." (Hebrews 11:24, 25) The second is the Messiah's resurrection cry of Psalm 16:11, showing where true pleasures lie: "Thou wilt show me the path of life: in thy presence is fulness of joy; at thy right hand there are pleasures for evermore."

Thus throughout our lives these three, cares, riches and pleasures are always at hand, in ground where they are native and flourish, that is our natural hearts, ready to strangle the Word, and bring to nothing its intended effect in the Kingdom of God.

In the last case study of this parable, the immeasurable powers of the Word of God when unhindered are demonstrated. "He that received seed into the good ground is he that heareth the word, and understandeth it; which also beareth fruit, and bringeth forth, some an hundredfold, some sixty, some thirty." (Matthew 13:23) It is not easy to be sure what is intended by the hundred, sixty and thirty. In Mark, the order is reversed, and in Luke, only the hundredfold is mentioned. In this hundred, sixty and thirtyfold, some have seen fruit for God in the Church, in Israel, and in the nations. There seems to be, however, little warrant for this, and it is perhaps most natural to take the figures as true to experience, but unimportant for the purpose of the parable, possibly referring to different capacities of individuals. In this case there would be a parallel with the later parable of the talents, where the words occur, "to every man according to his several ability."

In the case just mentioned, there might be some indication of degrees of 'goodness' in the good ground. But it would be much more natural to concentrate attention on the essential facts of the parable, according to which good ground would be defined as ground not trodden hard like the way side, not mixed with stones and so shallow, and not containing thorns as either plants or seeds allowed to grow undisturbed. This would rightly concentrate attention on the practical lesson that good ground is prepared and tended ground.

In one sense the preparation of the hearer is the work of God, and we see this most extensively illustrated in the Acts. In another sense, especially for the disciple, preparation for hearing the Word, and the tending required after hearing the Word are our responsibility. It is open to the disciple never to read or to hear the Word without lifting the heart to God, recognising the possibilities open, and praying that the Word may on each occasion accomplish within us what God desires. In the daily exercises of godliness we can give root and depth to the growth which is of God, even in the presence of affliction; we can root out the native shoots of cares, riches and pleasures.

The parable of the sower is of immeasurable importance to the lives of those who are seeking first the Kingdom. As a kind of extension to the parable itself rather than its interpretation, Spurgeon said: "You may omit, O recording angel, the fact that a warrior went forth to fight; it is far more important that you should record that "a sower went forth to sow." You may even forget that a man of science went into his laboratory and made a discovery, for no discovery can equal in importance the usual processes of husbandry. Do you hear the song of the harvest home? Do you see the loaded wagons follow one another to the farmer's barn? If so, remember that there would be no harvest home if the sower went not forth to sow. As the flail is falling upon the wheat, or the threshing machine is making the grain to leap from among the chaff, and the miller's wheels are grinding merrily, and the women are kneading the dough, and the bread is set upon the table, and parents and children are fed to the full, do not forget that all this could never happen unless "a sower went forth to sow." On this action hinges the very life of man. Bread, which is the staff of his life, would be broken, and taken from him, and his life could not continue did not a sower still go forth to sow."

When the time was fulfilled, and God turned to do a new thing in the world, and set about the introduction of the long-promised Kingdom, the action taken was that the Son of Man went forth to sow the Word. And the first great character stamped upon that Kingdom in the form it takes between the Comings is that the appointed instrument for its beginning and its progress is the preaching of the Word of God. To seek that Kingdom is to hear and to use that Word aright. Every time the Word of God is read, preached, or heard, the parable of the sower is being re-enacted in microcosm. The same evil one is at work; the same sinister and baleful influences are found; but the word of God received and understood, is powerful to form the Kingdom, to bring every thought into subjection to Christ.

It is at first sight a strange and unexpected thing that the Word should be less than universally successful, but it is true to experience, and not more strange than the existence of evil in the world. Thanks be to God it is also true to experience that the Word is extending its triumphs throughout the world, and for the purposes introductory to the New Testament epistles, it is plain that the reason is that the whole power of the grace of God and the operations of His Spirit are included in the concept of the Word at work in the hearts of men.

Chapter 9

PREACHING THE WORD

The sowing of the seed of the Word of God occupies so central a position in spreading the Kingdom in its present form, that it will be profitable to devote further thought to it. A study of the preaching of the Word in the Acts will be found to shed an instructive light on this point, revealing on every page how the parable of the sower was worked out in detail in the first days.

In the story of the Acts there are in operation four parties: the Word, the Preacher, the Hearer, and in all and through all, God. The Word, the Preacher, and the Hearer illustrate respectively the Seed, the Sower, (under Christ), and the Ground. Only when these three are in proper co-operation with and under God, are the hearers brought into the Kingdom.

The Word.
In this book of Scripture, the Word is spoken of as a thing of living energy. The Word grew (6:7. 12:24. 19:20), multiplied (12:24), spread itself (13:49), prevailed (19:20). Like seed it grows and multiplies, and by multiplying it spreads and has in itself the power to get the victory. This living activity of the Word first appears in Acts 6. When the apostles gave themselves to prayer and the ministry of the Word, then "the Word of God increased; and the number of the disciples multiplied in Jerusalem greatly; and a great company of the priests were obedient to the faith". Herod Agrippa I was an able and influential king, brought up in Rome as an intimate of the imperial family. In Acts 20:21 he was probably about to proclaim himself Emperor of the East in Caesarea, and on a set day he appeared in such dazzling splendour that his audience acclaimed his speech as the voice of a god. At that moment the angel of the Lord intervened again and smote him so that he died of a loathsome and horrible disease. Thus came to a full stop the plans by which his power was to grow, multiply, spread and prevail — **but**, "the Word of God grew and multiplied". In the next chapter is preserved the address given by Paul in the synagogue in Pisidian Antioch. At first many Jews believed, but when, on the next sabbath almost the whole city came together to hear the Word of God, the Jews were filled with envy, and as they rejected the Word, their refusal became the occasion of Paul's turning to the Gentiles and so "the Word of God spread itself abroad throughout the whole region". After

spending three months in the synagogue at Ephesus speaking of the things concerning the Kingdom of God (Acts 19), Paul based his ministry for a further two years on the lecture-hall of Tyrannus. From this place all in Asia heard the Word, and striking signs accompanied it. It proved itself superior to sickness and demon-possession, to vagabond Jews and curious arts — "so mightily grew the Word of God and prevailed".

The manner in which this vigorous and effective influence was let loose and spread abroad appears to have two main facets. The first fulfils the command to go out, and seeks out the places where the crowds of all sorts and conditions of men can be contacted in a listening mood, places such as synagogues and market-places. As for the second facet, interested hearers are separated and given further instruction for longer periods, as in the case just mentioned, when Paul separated the disciples and taught them daily in the lecture-hall of Tyrannus. To these two facets correspond the two main classes of words descriptive of the activity of the preachers. On the one hand they were heralds, making a public proclamation in the name of the highest authority, that of God. On the other hand the Word was taught and reasoned.

What exactly was the Word which manifested such power and produced such happy results? The Bible is, of course, the Word of God; and the Son is Himself the Word who was in the beginning with God. In the narrative of the Acts, it appears that the Word of God combines the two ideas. "Preach the Word", writes Paul to Timothy, "Be instant in season and out of season," and there can be no doubt what was the Word which they preached. They preached Christ out of the Scriptures. That all-glorious Name was the sum and substance of their message. The reason for the great joy which came to Samaria is described in two parallel phrases. "Philip went down to the city of Samaria and preached Christ unto them, and the people with one accord gave heed." (8:5) Then, (v.14) "the apostles which were at Jerusalem heard that Samaria had received the Word of God". To give heed to the preaching of Christ is to receive the Word of God. Preaching the Word of God is preaching Christ. The next part of the history takes Philip down to the southern desert, where he meets the eunuch returning from Jerusalem and reading the prophet Isaiah. The place of the Scripture which he read was "He was led as a sheep to the slaughter", and beginning at that Scripture Philip preached unto him Jesus. Philip took his stand on a passage of the Word which is the Bible, and preached unto him the Word which is Jesus. The fullest account of Paul's synagogue addresses is that mentioned earlier, the record in Acts 13 of his discourse at Antioch in Pisidia, but the theme is summarised most tersely in 17:3, the account of another synagogue address in Thessalonica. There he "reasoned with them out of the Scriptures, opening and alleging" two things: first, "that Messiah must needs have suffered, and risen again from the dead"; and second, "that this Jesus, whom I preach unto you, is Messiah".

A central feature of all the preaching of Christ in the Acts is the witness of the Resurrection. Once and again "they preached through Jesus the resurrection from the dead" (4:2); "with great power gave the apostles witness of the resurrection of the Lord Jesus" (4:33); "he preached unto them Jesus, and the resurrection" (17:18).

Such was the message by which the world was turned upside down; by which great joy was brought to cities; by which the worship of false gods was overthrown; by which haughty Pharisees and strangers from distant lands were brought to the feet of Jesus; by which the Lord added daily to the Church such as were being saved.

The question is worth asking; What is the message you preach from the pulpit or in the Sunday School, and from what source did you get it? Many preach what they have heard others preach, and this may be good in result, but it may not! The message we preach should be the Word of God, and whatever help we may receive from others, it should come immediately from God through the written Word. Others will really help us insofar as they lead us to receive the message ourselves from this pure fountain. "The Lord gave the Word: great was the number of those that published it." "Not unto us, O Lord, not unto us, but unto Thy name give glory, for Thy mercy and for Thy truth's sake".

The Hearer.

On 14th. October 1735 John Wesley committed to his diary that in company with his brother Charles and a few friends, he took ship from Gravesend in order to embark for Georgia to preach the gospel to the Indians. He continues, "our end in leaving our native country, was...singly this, to save our souls." In February 1738 he returned to England, very much disillusioned with the outcome so far, of the long and arduous process of labouring to save his soul. "It is now two years and almost four months since I left my native country in order to teach the Georgian Indians the nature of Christianity; but what have I learned myself in the meantime? Why (what I least of all suspected), that I who went to America to convert others, was never myself converted to God". A few days later (on a day "much to be remembered") he fell in with a Moravian, Peter Böhler, from whom he soon began to learn the futility of his scheme of salvation as the result of a long and arduous discipline. On a subsequent meeting with Peter Böhler, Wesley writes, "I had now no objection to what he said of the nature of faith...Neither could I deny the happiness or holiness he described, as the fruits of this living faith...But I could not comprehend what he spoke of an instantaneous work. I could not understand how this faith should be given in a moment; how a man could at once be thus turned from darkness to light, from sin and misery to righteousness and joy in the Holy Ghost. I searched the Scriptures again, touching this very thing, particularly the Acts of the Apostles. But, to my amazement, found scarce any instances there of other than instantaneous conversions." If, two hundred and forty or more years later we tread in the steps of John Wesley, and search the Acts to see whether these things are so, do we find that Wesley was right? It is true, of course, that in contrast with the idea of salvation by works, at the end of a long process of self-discipline, then instantaneous conversions are found in Scripture. But what is equally true, Wesley did not note at the time, that there is scarcely a case of conversion recorded in the Acts where there is not a (sometimes lengthy) process of **preparation**. It is at this point that we run alongside the parable of the sower, where so great an importance is attached to the preparedness of the ground. We must dwell on this preparation of the hearer, about to come to the moment of saving faith in Christ, and particularly to see how this preparation bears all the marks of being distinctly above the level of what can be planned or achieved by any merely human agency. In the majority of cases the process of preparation of the hearer is more hinted at than described, but these delicate touches leave no doubt at all of its existence. In the case of Saul of Tarsus, he had been subjected to the persuasion of the goads — "it is hard for thee to kick against the pricks". When Paul came to the riverside at Philippi, he found there Lydia, "whose heart the Lord had opened", so that she was prepared to attend to the Word. These evidences of the ubiquity of a prior work in those who, on hearing, received the Word, give the greater weight to those instances in the earlier chapters, in which the preparation is minutely described, and shown to be effectuated often by agencies different and distant from, and indeed unknown to the persons through whom the hearer was brought to final decision. And with this agree those other Scriptures where **birth** by water and the Spirit clearly implies a process prior to the instant of saving faith and entrance into the light of life.

    The preparation of the Ethiopian eunuch began more than a thousand miles away from the scene of his conversion, in Meroë, where the rulers of Ethiopia held court. In that distant land the eunuch's heart was reached by the power of the Scriptures, read in the synagogues, sufficiently to bring him to the home of the Old Testament, Jerusalem, to offer his worship. Returning from Jerusalem in his chariot, he was already reading one of the greatest of those Old Testament Scriptures which testify beforehand of the sufferings of Christ and the glory that should follow. He was filled with an enquiring hunger for a greater knowledge of the Sufferer there described: "He was led as a sheep to the slaughter; and like a lamb dumb before his shearer, so opened he not his mouth." He was as exactly ready for the preaching of Christ as it is possible to imagine, and so it is small wonder that he gladly received the Word, and went on his way rejoicing. The custodian of the queen's treasure returned to her court the possessor of wealth beyond all earthly store. Equally clear is the fact of the preparation of Cornelius for hearing and receiving the Word. When he first appears in 10:2, he is already in one sense a prepared man. He can only have become devout and God-fearing and devoted to prayer and almsgiving under the influence of the Scriptures. He seems to have been consciously expecting that in answer to his prayers God would eventually grant some signal message from Himself. It was to a

Gentile thus waiting for God that the Word came, "Send for one Simon, whose surname is Peter, he shall tell thee what thou oughtest to do." Thus it came about that when Peter opened his mouth and preached the Word, he was speaking to men and women already hungering for all things commanded by God.

Does this kind of preparation of the hearer, on a plane quite outside the possibility of mere human arrangement, occur today? Everyone with experience of conversions knows that it is so. One example from within my own experience must suffice to illustrate the point. A few years ago there lived in a certain town in the North of England a man of about thirty years of age, by upbringing a church member, and therefore accustomed to hearing the Scriptures read. But he came to realise that he did not really believe in God, and that this anomalous position would have to be faced. He decided to live as though he did believe in God, and see how it worked out. In this 'faith' he lived for several years, continuing as a church member, and even found some victory over temptations to drink. He was eventually brought to a more definite decision, which was to live as a Christian, that is, to read the Bible and pray, and about this time became a lay-preacher. He was a bachelor, living with a sister and her husband, and he used to gather a group of friends in their house to read the Bible and pray. Thus was formed a little cell of men and women, devout, fearing God, and praying to God alway. The lay-preacher's brother-in-law fell seriously ill and was face to face with death; he recovered, however, and during his convalescence the lay-preacher procured for him Dorothy Sayers' "The Man Born to be King". Husband and wife read this book together, and it greatly influenced them. On Easter Sunday they were able to walk to church together, and experienced a strange feeling that they were walking together on 'the Calvary road'. At this juncture they all listened to the gospel clearly and faithfully preached every evening for a week. They were all converted almost immediately; last of all the lay-preacher. Up to this moment, they had never heard of the need to receive Christ for salvation.

These thoughts should prepare us for the realisation, if we have not realised it before, that the real and ultimate worker in the Acts is God. At a first reading, it might appear that the book is arranged on the basis that in the earlier chapters Peter is the worker, and he eventually gives way to Paul, as the instrument for the revelation of what completes the word of God. All this is true, in the sense that God uses Peter and Paul as His workmen, but the Person really at work is God, and to this theme we must now turn attention. It might be felt that such considerations take us outside the direct bearing of the parable of the sower, but they are unquestionably relevant to any discussion of the Kingdom of God.

"God which worketh all in all"
The pages of the Acts bear the marks of the most astonishingly exact

co-ordination of all the agencies concerned. The stage is certainly being set, and the scenes managed; but not by men, even men of God. God is behind the scenes, and is moving them Himself. There is no other conceivable explanation for this perfect co-ordination of all the parts. It might be objected to the point of view being taken here, that to organise is part of our contemporary world, and that it was not part of the world of the New Testament. Anyone with knowledge of the Roman world knows how far this is from the truth. There can be no question that the inspired author of the Acts was well acquainted with the elaborate degree of organisation existing and operating in the Roman world. The supply and movement of armies, the corn supply for the city of Rome, the collection of taxes, the administration of the provinces, were only possible because of the genius for organisation available. In the work of the gospel simple and rudimentary arrangements were made of course, as in the school of Tyrannus, but the gospel did not rely on organisation, not because they did not know how to organise, but because they knew a "more excellent way", which we would do well to learn.

The management of the scenes and the setting of the stage are convenient headings under which to look again at the Acts to see how clearly the Person at work is God himself. The former is on the surface for all to see, the latter requires a rather closer observation.

The Scenes Managed. The three agencies at work under God in the Acts were noted at the outset: the Word, the Hearer, and the Preacher. In the preceding paragraphs it became evident that Hearers were being prepared, and that it was God who was preparing them. There was no element of chance in the marking out of the persons who would believe. If we now review the same narratives it will also become manifest that the bringing together of Hearer and Preacher was dictated by God, deploying nothing less than omniscience in doing so. Can there be any man-made substitute for this?

Taking the same outstanding examples in the order in which they occur in the Acts, the case of the eunuch comes first. Immediately following the exciting and even dramatic events connected with Philip, Samaria and Simon, "the angel of the Lord spake unto Philip, saying, 'Arise and go toward the south unto the way that goeth down from Jerusalem unto Gaza, which is desert.' And he arose and went." God is now managing the scene, and quite independently of, and superior to the knowledge of His servant. The eunuch had to travel more than a thousand miles, with the luxury of his chariot and a train of attendants. Philip had to finish with one great work of God, and to travel seventy or eighty miles, evidently on foot. They met at the exact moment for the eunuch's blessing, for so it had been ordained of God, and the really crucial matter was that His servant's ear and will were so tuned in that he was simply and instantly at God's disposal.

In the histories of the conversion of Saul and Cornelius, the servants of God manifested some reluctance, in the one case due to very understandable fear, and in the other due to equally understandable Judaistic prejudice. In each case there is the same delightful directness of communication between our ever-patient God and His reluctant servant, reminiscent of patriarchal times. The coincidence of events, if attributed to chance, would be unbelievably astonishing. When the messengers of Cornelius set out on their journey, Peter was of a mind in which he would have shown them the door. When they arrived at Joppa, a prepared Peter received them kindly. We should not lose the full wonder of the coincidence because we can see so clearly that the worker was God.

A rather different aspect of the matter is illustrated in the history of Paul up to the point of his special commission for the work of the Lord in 13:2. There is no trace of an idea that Paul planned for himself a kind of 'career' in the gospel. After his conversion and contact with the apostles in Jerusalem, his action is most interesting. He does a very humdrum-looking thing, that is, he simply goes home to Tarsus (9:30) and there remains until (11:25) Barnabas comes to Tarsus to bring him to help in the new work at Antioch. There he continued in the ordinary course of assembly life until (13:2) the Holy Ghost, by prophecy, separated him for the great work for which God thus called him. The same principle is to be observed in the life and work of Luther. He seems to have had no idea of planning the immense achievements now universally linked with his name. After his conversion, from the moment when he was so outraged by the sale of indulgences that he nailed his theses to the door of the church at Wittenberg, he faced each situation as it arose, and in this way God led him step by step until the great work was done.

The Stage Set. It is easy to overlook, (although it is an often-told story), that God is not only managing the scenes, but is doing so on a stage set by Himself. It was "in the fulness of the time" that God sent forth His Son. It was "in due time" that Christ died for the ungodly. Wherever Paul and his company journeyed preaching the Word, things were prepared for them in that they found ready:

> meeting places for Jews and prepared Gentiles — synagogues;
> a common language — Greek;
> the Greek Bible;
> ease of travel over many countries.

The fact that the messengers of the gospel found **synagogues** nearly everywhere was due to the Jewish Dispersion, to which several references are made in Scripture (John 7:35, 1 Peter 1:1, James 1:1). A modern historian, unlikely to have much interest in emphasizing the providential preparation of the world for the spread of the gospel, writes: "The most remarkable phenomenon presented by Judaism in the Graeco-Roman period is its dispersion along the shores of the Mediterranean". Probably we have to look for the commencement of the process with the Jews who remained in Babylon at the time of the return of the Remnant under Zerubbabel and

Jeshua, but even in those early days the process seems to have been on a wider scale, since there was a military colony of Jewish mercenaries in the time of Nehemiah located at Elephantine in Egypt. Movements of Jews to Egypt are often witnessed by Isaiah and Jeremiah. Probably the most important movements for our purpose took place in the sections into which the realms of Alexander the Great fell apart after his death in B.C.323. Since relations with God's people were mainly in the hands of two of these successors, they are singled out in Scripture for special mention as the King of the North (the Seleucids, reigning in their principal city of Antioch in Syria), and the King of the South (the Ptolemies, reigning in their principal city of Alexandria in Egypt). During the fluctuating fortunes of these two dynasties the Jews were spread far and wide around the Mediterranean coast from Rome through Greece, Asia Minor and Syria to Egypt. Among these widely dispersed settlements of Jews the Pharisees organised and developed the synagogues in the second century B.C.

These communities of Jews were not small in numbers or importance. Their number in Egypt in the time of Christ was estimated at one million. They everywhere made a powerful impact, and many Gentile proselytes or God-fearers were numbered among the regular synagogue congregations. Thus we find in the Acts that the Pauline party found everywhere ready-made audiences, first of Jews, but always giving immediate access to Gentiles divinely prepared for the reception of the gospel of Christ.

It is often overlooked that even the Epistle to the Romans was written, not in Latin, but in the **Greek language,** and this is a striking instance of the immense importance of the existence of a universal language in the world where the first preachers travelled. It was, of course, the conquests of Alexander which spread abroad the Greek language in this way. In the process, the classical language of Plato became modified for everyday use, and one of the most interesting modern discoveries has been papyri preserved in Egypt containing records of everyday transactions. These not only show the extent to which the Greek language had become 'domesticated', throughout the world, but also furnish important illustrations of the contemporary meanings of New Testament words. The result of all this was that a knowledge of the Greek language would take a traveller anywhere in the civilised world. The language question is important in the Acts. "Canst thou speak Greek?" said the chief captain in Acts 21:37, and the narrative glides easily over the facility with which Paul switched from speaking Greek to the chief captain to addressing the crowd of Jews in Aramaic. To contemplate the language problem of today in the same area, and consider a land journey round the eastern shores of the Mediterranean from Egypt to Rome or Spain, reveals a very great contrast, not to the advantage of the present day. All this was not by chance, but was an element in God's working, leading up to the "fulness of time".

The language question, greatly important for preaching, is yet more important because it made possible the **Greek Bible**. We have seen that the Word they preached was 'Christ out of the Scriptures', and now we observe that the audiences were composed in the synagogues of Jews and Gentiles who knew the Scriptures and understood and received such addresses as that given in Pisidian Antioch. (Acts 13) The natural outcome, (and yet so much more than natural), of the facts of the Jewish Dispersion and the spread of the Greek language had been the translation of the Old Testament into Greek about 200 years before Christ. This took place at Alexandria in Egypt, and since it was the work of seventy-two elders, it was called the Septuagint (LXX). This was the book being read by the eunuch. This was the book in the hands of the synagogue audiences in Antioch, Corinth, Ephesus, and so many other cities named.

Among the works which the world of the New Testament owed, under God, to the Romans, as distinct from the Greeks, in the subjects of the preceding paragraphs, was the "majesty of the Roman peace" and **the Roman roads**. This is as well exemplified in Britain as anywhere else. Right until the advent of the motorways, which deliberately set out to avoid cities, the main roads of England follow the network of roads made by the Romans. It is rather striking that while there is a good deal of reference in Acts to ease of sea travel, road travel seems to be taken for granted, until we come to the Appian Way suggested in 28:15 and well-known today to every visitor. Apart from seasonal delays due to weather, it seems to have been the easiest thing in the world to book a sea passage. Ease and security of travel was no small element in the providential preparation for the preaching of the gospel. The "perils of robbers" noted in 2 Corinthians 11:26 were indeed real sufferings, but they did not prevent travel.

The sum of these particular facts is that it is beyond human power to arrange things on the scale (in both time and space) in which God orders them. What really matters is not to have a wide-spreading organisation, but to give absolute priority to being available to God for the work which He is surely doing, so that His servants may be set each in his place to act for God as He ordains.

The Preacher.

Our present reading of the Acts will have failed in its purpose if it has not awakened the question: How can I be available to God for the work He is unfailingly carrying out? If we are seeking the Kingdom of God we shall certainly wish to ask this question.

A Vessel fit for the Master's Use. 2 Timothy 2:14-26 deals with this question and especially vv. 20 and 21. "But in a great house there are not only vessels of gold and of silver, but also of wood and of earth; and some to honour, and some to dishonour. If a man therefore purge himself from these, he shall be a vessel unto honour, sanctified, and meet for the master's use," The picture presented here is of the instruments, utensils and tools available in a large house. Because it is a large house several persons will be requiring the use of utensils, for example the servants, the family, and the master. In such a case there will be a sharp distinction between the utensils and tools for everyone to use, and the utensils "fit for the master". In many a modern home, woe betide nine-year-old Peter if he thinks that father's best wood-chisel is suitable for Peter to hack away at his boat! The exact picture coming to us from the ancient world through Paul's page is that of the distinction between the possibly earthenware vessels suitable only for the lowly and even degraded use of the slaves, and the gold and silver "fit for the master", to shine at his table and do him honour. And here we have reached the writer's point of emphasis. We want to know what makes a vessel fit for the Master.

Throughout the Bible we meet the truth that the instruments God uses are not primarily methods, but men and women consecrated to Him. Good methods without good men are useless to God; and the right men will use the right methods. The order, in the scale of availability and usefulness to God is first, consecrated men and women (and therefore filled with the Holy Spirit), and afterwards good methods as He guides them. Through the Bible story we read of the great succession of men and women who have been God's instruments: Moses, Joshua, Gideon, Deborah, Jeremiah, Priscilla and Aquila, and so many others. How can I be in this great succession of men and women available to God? Vessels of gold and silver will shine, as we have said, but in this case they shine for the Master, and show forth His glory. Close to each other in Westminster Abbey are two tablets. One, by far the larger, is on the wall ostensibly to honour Milton, but, alas, out of a dozen or so lines, only two refer to Milton, and all the rest show forth the praises of — the man who paid for the tablet! Close by, in the floor, is a small stone, and there is scarcely a visitor to the Abbey who has not heard its fame and does not look for it. It contains only four words: "O rare Ben Jonson." We are moved to repeat: "Not unto us, O Lord, not unto us, but unto Thy Name give glory."

A Cleaned-out Vessel. Our verse describes the vessel unto honour in both negative and positive terms. Negatively, it is a purged vessel, a vessel which has been cleaned out. It is not sufficient to be a vessel of gold or silver. It must be cleaned out also, and only if this is done will it be a vessel fit for the master. If it has not been cleaned out he will put it down and call for another! The cleaning out is negative, a separating of all that is evil. The terms of this passage indicate that the first meaning of the cleaning out is purging away all association with teachers of evil doctrine. Examples of the evil teaching are given in the preceding verses: striving about words to no effect; profane and vain babblings; saying that the resurrection is past already. v.22 shows that a moral cleansing is also in mind. In John 13 the Lord teaches us that a disciple who has undergone the once-for-all cleansing also requires oft-repeated washing. The once-for-all cleansing is perhaps analagous to being a vessel of silver or gold. The oft-repeated cleansing may be likened to the cleaning-out of a vessel to renew its fitness for the Master.

Psalm 66:28 raises the question of what we regard in our hearts, and Psalm 51 prays, "Create in me a clean heart, O God; and renew a right spirit within me". Ignatius Loyola, emerging from a religious retreat, was seen to be so chastened and alarmed that his companions asked what he had been shown, "a cage of devils"? He replied, "Worse than that, they showed me my heart." The epistles to Timothy name many uncleannesses which can be regarded in the heart: covetousness, strife, youthful lusts. In passing from 2 Corinthians 6:17 to 7:1, Paul passes from the need for a positional separation to a spiritual cleansing. "Let us cleanse ourselves from all filthiness of the flesh and spirit, perfecting holiness in the fear of God". If action requires adjustment, then it is because the heart needs cleaning out, and the agent for this cleaning out is ever and always the Word of God. At this point we are very distinctly in the same realm of thought as in the parable of the sower, the action of the Word in bringing about the establishment of the will of God. The cleansing is worked out by prayerful application to ourselves of the Word of God as we read it day by day. The Psalms are full of this dual action of the Word of God and prayer in the cleansing of the saints. The Psalms are themselves the prayers, and within them is contained the application to himself by the Psalmist of God's law. Psalm 19:7-14 is a great example. The perfect law of the Lord converts the soul: the pure commandment of the Lord enlightens the eyes: the clean fear of the Lord endures for ever: yet are they "more to be desired than gold,...sweeter also than honey". In the end he applies all this to himself and his errors in prayer: "Cleanse thou me from secret faults...Let the words of my mouth, and the meditation of my heart, be acceptable in thy sight, O Lord, my strength and my redeemer".

A Sanctified Vessel. The vessel unto honour is described positively in that it is a sanctified vessel, that is, separated (not only **from** evil, but) "unto the Lord". As we know, sanctification in Scripture is often the action of God's Spirit as a result of which a person believes (1 Peter 1:2), or the sanctification by the will of God, through the offering of the body of Jesus Christ once for all (Hebrews 10:10). In other cases it describes a feature of the actual life of the Christian for which prayer is made. "Sanctify them through thy truth: thy word is truth...And for their sakes I sanctify myself, that they also might be sanctified through the truth" (John 17: 17, 19). "The very God of peace sanctify you wholly" (1 Thessalonians 5:23). It is in the latter sense that it is used here, and translated into well-known phrases, it means that only if I am out and out, wholeheartedly out and out, am I available for the Master. Two young men were conducting a preaching campaign, and one remarked in an address that some Christians want to be all head and others all heart. It is better (he said) to be evenly balanced. Afterwards the other commented, with some glee, "I was delighted with your definition of the ideal Christian — half-hearted and half-witted!" We are not often satisfied with being thought half-witted, but too often we know very well that we are only half-hearted in serving the Lord. The great lesson of the Books of Kings is that as David followed the Lord "with a whole heart", so the only way of true prosperity is to do the same. In the Kingdom of God, wholehearted and exclusive dedication to the Lord and His service is the sanctification which is indispensable if we are to be fit for the Master's use. And this is brought about by the constraining power of the love of Christ, realised ever afresh in the believer's heart.

> *I'd look to Him till sight endear*
> *The Saviour to my heart;*
> *To Him I look who calms my fear,*
> *Nor from Himself would part.*
>
> *I'd look until His precious love*
> *My every thought control,*
> *Its vast constraining influence prove*
> *O'er body, spirit, soul.*

Prayer. Returning finally to the story of the Acts, what is the predominant character of those who are found so outstandingly usable by God? What is the habitual attitude in which the conditions outlined in the preceding paragraphs are most powerfully encouraged? The servant fit for the Master's use, cleaned out, and sanctified, is found to be a praying servant. This waiting on God, this awareness of His holiness, this power of His love, are realised through prayer. When, in the Acts, men and women are found available to God for the work He was doing, they were men and women of prayer, and, indeed, often at the moment engaged in prayer. A concordance of the Acts would cause praying to stand out as a dominant activity.

Someone has remarked that when some problem, obstacle, or distress fell upon any of their number, the disciples "simply rushed to prayer". Especially note their prayer when assembled in 4:24-31. "And when they had prayed, the place was shaken where they were assembled together; and they were all filled with the Holy Ghost, and they spake the word of God with boldness". In 12:5, when Peter was in prison, "prayer was made without ceasing of the church unto God for him." Especially also we shall wish to note how often the same theme recurs concerning individuals: the apostles (6:4,6), Peter (9:40, 8:15, 10:9) Paul (9:11, 16:25, 28:8), Cornelius (10:2,30), the Church at Antioch (13:3). In the story as we have found it in the Acts, these are the individuals found available to God for the work in which He was engaged.

At the beginning of this chapter, in which we have illustrated the parable of the sower from the Acts, four parties to the work of preaching the Word were distinguished; God, the Word, the Hearer, and the Preacher. God cannot fail: His Word never changes or loses its power: the Kingdom of God is forwarded, when the preacher is available to God, a vessel fit for the

Master's use. It is for the Lord's servants, therefore, by ceaseless, importunate, prevailing prayer to seek the Lord's help to fulfil this condition.

MATTHEW 13:24 to 43

24 Another parable put he forth unto them, saying, The kingdom of
25 heaven is likened unto a man which sowed good seed in his field: But while men slept, his enemy came and sowed tares among the wheat, and
26 went his way. But when the blade was sprung up, and brought forth
27 fruit, then appeared the tares also. So the servants of the householder came and said unto him, Sir, didst not thou sow good seed in thy field?
28 from whence then hath it tares? He said unto them, An enemy hath done this. The servants said unto him, Wilt thou then that we go and
29 gather them up? But he said, Nay; lest while ye gather up the tares, ye
30 root up also the wheat with them. Let both grow together until the harvest: and in the time of harvest I will say to the reapers, Gather ye together first the tares, and bind them in bundles to burn them: but
31 gather the wheat into my barn. Another parable put he forth unto them, saying, The kingdom of heaven is like to a grain of mustard seed,
32 which a man took, and sowed in his field: Which indeed is the least of all seeds: but when it is grown, it is the greatest among herbs, and becometh a tree, so that the birds of the air come and lodge in the
33 branches thereof. Another parable spake he unto them; The kingdom of heaven is like unto leaven, which a woman took, and hid in three
34 measures of meal, till the whole was leavened. All these things spake Jesus unto the multitude in parables; and without a parable spake he
35 not unto them: That it might be fulfilled which was spoken by the prophet, saying, I will open my mouth in parables; I will utter things
36 which have been kept secret from the foundation of the world. Then Jesus sent the multitude away, and went into the house: and his disciples came unto him, saying, Declare unto us the parable of the tares of the
37 field. He answered and said unto them, He that soweth the good seed is
38 the Son of man; The field is the world; the good seed are the children
39 of the kingdom; but the tares are the children of the wicked one; The enemy that sowed them is the devil; the harvest is the end of the world;
40 and the reapers are the angels. As therefore the tares are gathered and
41 burned in the fire; so shall it be in the end of this world. The Son of man shall send forth his angels, and they shall gather out of his
42 kingdom all things that offend, and them which do iniquity; And shall cast them into a furnace of fire: there shall be wailing and gnashing of
43 teeth. Then shall the righteous shine forth as the sun in the kingdom of their Father. Who hath ears to hear, let him hear.

Chapter 10

EVIL IN THE KINGDOM

The three parables which follow the parable of the sower have for their subject the positive working of evil in the Kingdom of heaven. Who, listening to the words of the Lord, and seeing His mastery of evil as shown in His works would expect that evil could ever flourish in Christianity? and who, reading these three parables of the Kingdom of heaven, can in the event be surprised at the frightening confusion manifested in the Christianity of our times? For we must constantly bear in mind that the seven parables of Matthew 13 are the first comprehensive account of Christianity as to its course and development between the first and second advents of Christ. Within this systematic account, the purpose of the parables of the tares, of the mustard, seed, and of the leaven, is to announce solemnly the fact that evil, as well as good, would find an entrance into the Kingdom, that its development would be monstrous, and that it would permeate the whole. On what foundation can any hope be based that a worthwhile result will in the end issue from this mass of confusion? The certainty of a supremely worthwhile result stems from the knowledge that God is at work by His Word. The whole marvel of the grace of God and His Spirit's action is centred in these parables at this one point, that the Word of the Kingdom is, where received and understood, surely producing fruit for God. This is the foundation laid in the first parable (the sower) and repeated and confirmed in the second (the tares).

The parable of the tares among the wheat covers a defined period of time which plainly and obviously embraces the entire interval between the first and the second comings; and it is the only one of the seven parables to do so. It is also the first of the seven to be explicitly described as a likeness of the Kingdom. The parable begins with the Son of Man sowing the good seed, and ends with the end of the age. Embedded in this disclosure of the apparently invincible rise and spread of the devil's work, is the assurance of One who knows the end from the beginning. The same Son of Man who begins the good work will unravel the tangled growth in His own time, and make the crooked straight; and then shall the righteous shine forth as the sun in the Kingdom of their Father. At first sight there is a substantial difference between the meaning of the seed in the parable of the sower and in this parable of the tares. "The good seed are the children of the kingdom." The attempt has been made to interpret this literally, by saying that the good seed and the tares are not messages preached and spread, but persons providentially scattered here and there over the same areas of the world. It seems to me more natural to take the seed in the same sense as in the first parable, and thus, by a familiar figure of speech, give the name of the effect to the agent producing the effect. If this view be accepted, then verse 24 together with its interpretation in verses 37 and 38 places the sowing alongside the sowing of the Word of God in the parable of the sower, and the children of the Kingdom are the fruit it produces.

The new light provided by the Lord in this parable is that an enemy, the devil, took occasion by the lack of watchfulness in the Kingdom to sow the seeds of positive evil. In a later parable of the Kingdom of heaven, the ten virgins, our attention is drawn to this same sleep. "While the bridegroom tarried, they all slumbered and slept." We are here brought face to face with the fact that the enemy's work is in our midst. "Many false prophets are gone out into the world." (1 John 4:1) The sombre fact has to be faced; the damage has never been undone; to the end of the chapter we have always to reckon with the presence of evil among us. Efforts directed to rooting out the evil are expressly forbidden; and how true it has been that when, in the hands of the Inquisition, it was claimed that the attempt was made to do just this, they did indeed root out and burn many thousands of the true children of the Kingdom. It is ordained that once the tares have been sown, both shall grow together until the harvest.

At this point the question is bound to arise whether this parable demands the abrogation in the church of the power of binding and loosing, of discipline in receiving to and rejection from the fellowship of the body of Christ. The answer must be an emphatic negative. What is here forbidden, as has already been noted, is what the Inquisition pretended, that is to root out and burn the children of the wicked one from among the wheat. The parable has, understood thus, a sufficiently full meaning, and cannot possibly be understood as cancelling beforehand the assembly discipline, only afterwards to be fully described in 1 Corinthians. I note the point here, but do not attempt to generalise upon it, that there is very little indeed said anywhere about internal relations in the Kingdom of heaven. If one ranges in thought over all the Kingdom references in gospels and epistles, only the parable of the two debtors in Matthew 18 appears to touch this point in its tremendous insistence on the obligation to mutual forgiveness. In contrast with this, when Scripture opens up the subject of the Church, then we have the fullest directions for its internal order and relationships and discipline. It is difficult to conceive how anyone, with this parable and its interpretation before them, can ever have believed the delusion that the Kingdom in its fulness will be brought about by the preaching of the Word. The good and the evil will grow together until the end, and only by the personal intervention of the Lord will all things that offend be gathered out of His Kingdom with burning and with destruction. As always, we need the light of prophecy, as a light shining in a dark place, to give the certainty that the tangled mass will be unravelled when, in the time of harvest, the Son of Man shall send forth His angels.

Putting together the parable and the interpretation, we can distinguish three events which will bring to an end the mixed condition of the Kingdom. These are, first the gathering of the tares and binding them into bundles; second, gathering the wheat into the barn of its heavenly home; and lastly gathering out of His Kingdom all things that offend, that is, the tares already bundled, and burning them. The outline sketched by these revelations leaves many details to be added in the later part of the New Testament. The essential revelation is that the transition from the present mixed condition to the yet future form when the knowledge of the Lord shall cover the earth as the waters cover the sea, will not be gradual, or by the eventual triumph of the Word itself, but by the catastrophic intervention of the Son of Man. He is indeed the Star of the coming day, and with the rising of the Sun of righteousness with healing in His wings, will be seen an earthly Kingdom from which all offence and iniquity will have been purged, and a celestial family shining forth "as the Sun in the Kingdom of their Father."

The parables of the mustard seed and the leaven are not interpreted by the Lord and we are accordingly confined to the light given by the Spirit of God in other Scriptures to enable us to seize their meaning. In the former of these the evil to be introduced into the Kingdom is seen in another light. Whereas in its beginning it would not be such as would make much stir in the world, in its result it was destined to astonish by its greatness. Here we have a clear addition to what has been learned from the parable of the tares. It might have been thought that the evil in the Kingdom would continue to occupy an insignificant position. We are here let into the secret beforehand that on the most public platform and on the scale of the powers of the nations, the evil element would be the one to assume a dominant role. The imagery employed by the Lord in this parable contains two elements which can easily be identified, and there can be little question that we are intended to make use of these parallel Scriptures to enable us to understand the tree. In Daniel's fourth chapter, there is found the account of one of Nebuchadnezzar's dreams. In it he saw a tree, which by a decree from heaven, was cut down, but eventually permitted to grow again. Daniel, being called in to interpret the dream, does so in the following words. "The tree that thou sawest, which grew, and was strong, whose height reached unto the heaven, and the sight thereof to all the earth; whose leaves were fair, and the fruit thereof much, and in it was meat for all; under which the beasts of the field dwelt, and upon whose branches the fowls of the heaven had their habitation: it is thou, O king, that art grown and become strong: for thy greatness is grown, and reacheth unto heaven, and thy dominion to the end of the earth." (Daniel 4: 20-22) From this we learn that the symbol of a tree means a great political system, which by its spreading harbours evil. It has already been made clear from the interpretation of the parable of the sower that the 'birds of the air' represent the activities of the Evil One.

The other Scripture bearing on the interpretation of the parable of the mustard seed is Revelation 17 and 18 dealing with Babylon the Great. There are two notes in chapter seventeen which make it absolutely certain that this Babylon is Rome or is centred on Rome. "The seven heads are seven mountains, on which the woman sitteth." (verse 9) and, "The woman ... is that great city, which reigneth over the kings of the earth." (verse 18) These two marks of identification could not conceivably, in the reign of Vespasian when they were given as the chapter itself records, point in any other direction than Rome. The pertinent verse is 18:2, "Babylon ... is become the habitation of devils, and the hold of every foul spirit, and a cage of every unclean and hateful bird." A description having its final meaning after Babylon's fall, this yet provides a striking parallel with the developed condition of the great tree arising from the mustard seed, where evil birds have their lodging.

I think we have to see the fulfilment of this prophecy in the present state of Christianity in the world, reckoned to be an influential part of the Establishment. We have to review in thought the patronage of Christianity by Constantine in the fourth century; the development of the Papal States and the temporal power claimed and exercised by the popes in the Middle Ages; and on to the secure position of Christianity as part of the modern Establishment in the West and in the lands developed from the West. A modern ecclesiastical historian has illustrated the development in the Middle Ages by a comparison of the achievements of the Popes Gregory 1 (A.D. 590) and Gregory V11 (A.D. 1073). "Gregory 1 claimed the spiritual primacy which descended to the vicar of Christ, the successor of S. Peter, but he wrote to the emperor at Constantinople in humility as a subject. Gregory V11 was to claim not merely supreme spiritual but supreme temporal power, to declare an emperor deposed, and to plunge Germany and Italy into war to enforce his will." (Deanesley). Passing over a millennium and coming to discussions of the contemporary scene, how often the sentence is heard, "Christianity has failed." In this familiar sentence, what meaning is implied for the word "Christianity"? Certainly not the lowly and humble body, in the world but not of it, and single-mindedly devoted to bearing the Name of a Christ in reproach and spreading His Word in the world. This is what is envisaged by the Church in the New Testament. Rather; in the contemporary dialogue, Christianity is the name given to an imposing and important part of the Establishment, and most obviously tending to be centred on Rome through the ecumenical movement. When it is said that Christianity has failed, the meaning implied or explicit is that it has failed to prevent war, to effect disarmament, or to solve the racial problem. A great deal might be said about what Christians have effected on these points and many other aspects of the human problem, but at the moment the point is that these objectives, in the political sense, were not included in the charge given to the true Church by Christ and His apostles, so that in its revolutionary power they turned the world upside down. When we spread the Word of the Lord, then, as at the beginning, great joy follows its reception, and those who believe enter the only real good, both for this life and for that life which is to come. Are our aspirations and efforts directed to eventuate in the fruit for God and man produced from the good seed, or are they beamed towards this monstrous tree, and to the tares, whose end is to be destroyed?

In approaching the parable of the leaven in the meal, the moment is perhaps opportune to take note of a feature which has caused difficulty. The parable begins, in verse 33, "The Kingdom of heaven is like unto leaven." Is the Kingdom likened to the leaven only, as distinct from being likened to the ensemble of meal and leaven, or indeed, to the whole action and its result? The question might well be widened. Is the Kingdom likened to the man who sowed the good seed, or to the entire process and the result? (verse 24) And the same question arises as to the grain of mustard seed, (verse 31) the treasure, (verse 44) the merchant man, (verse 45) or the net (verse 47). Many have racked their brains to reconcile the detail pin-pointed in each case, but I am sure that the answer lies elsewhere. We might imagine brackets as follows: "The kingdom of heaven is like unto (leaven, which a woman took, and hid in three measures, till the whole was leavened)." If this be the correct view, then the object (grammatically) of the verb and preposition "likened unto," is not the leaven, but the whole process and result as set out to the end of the parable, and similarly in the other parables.

The parable presents the process of diffusion throughout a mass in the guise of three measures of meal entirely permeated by leaven or yeast. Our method of study, as with the previous parable, is to look for light given by the Spirit of God in other Scriptures. It is soon discovered that preparing three measures of meal for food is by no means uncommon in the Old Testament. When the Lord, under the form of three men, visited Abraham, he "hastened into the tent unto Sarah, and said, Make ready quickly three measures of fine meal, knead it, and make cakes upon the hearth." Numbers 15:9 is one of many allusions to the Meat (or better, Meal) Offering. "Then shall he bring with a bullock a meal offering of three tenth deals of flour." This direction in Numbers 15 is distinguished by the increasing amount of meal, from one measure in verse 4, to two measures in verse 6, and finally three measures in verse 9. Thus three measures of meal is the full provision for God and His priests. (Leviticus 2:2,3) The woman's field of action is therefore the true bread for God and for His people, a matter of literally vital importance. What meaning was intended by the Lord for this leaven, put into the meal and then permeating the whole? If we wish to allow Scripture to interpret itself, we need only look at three passages to encompass the whole. The turning of a few pages will bring us to Matthew 16:12. "He bade them not beware of the leaven of bread, but of the **doctrine** of the Pharisees and of the Sadducees." Galatians 5:7-9. "Ye did run well; who did hinder you that ye should not obey the truth? This persuasion cometh not of Him that calleth you. A little leaven leaveneth the whole lump." These show that leaven is uniformly **doctrine**, and exclusively evil doctrine. The one remaining passage is 1 Corinthians 5:6 to 8. Here the phrase, "the leaven of malice and wickedness," presents the character and behaviour resulting from evil in doctrine. He is much less than a scribe instructed unto the Kingdom, who thinks that doctrine does not concern him.

Who or what is represented by the woman? It would be difficult to avoid the force of Revelation 2:20. "I have this against thee, that thou sufferest the woman Jezebel, which calleth herself a prophetess; and she teacheth and seduceth My servants to commit fornication." This brings us again inescapably to Rome. This point will be understood by those who see, amongst other meanings intended in the letters to the seven churches in Revelation 2 and 3, the identification of the church in Thyatira with Christendom in its Roman form, probably enlarged by the ecumenical movement, as the source of this most desperately sinister of all the aspects of evil in the Kingdom brought together in these three parables, that of corrupting the pure meal for the saint's nourishment. How thoroughly the devil's work in this respect has been performed, every true Christian knows. It is therefore all the more heartening to turn in the next parables to learn what there is for the heart of God, and therefore for His people in the field where the Word has been sown.

MATTHEW 13:44-46
44 Again, the kingdom of heaven is like unto treasure hid in a field; the which, when a man hath found, he hideth, and for joy thereof goeth and selleth all that he hath, and buyeth that field.
45 Again, the kingdom of heaven is like unto a merchantman,
46 seeking goodly pearls: Who, when he had found one pearl of great price, went and sold all that he had, and bought it.

Chapter 11

THE TREASURE AND THE PEARL

In the last three of the parables of the Kingdom in Matthew 13 there exists a problem of interpretation arising from two parallelisms. These are respectively the parables of the treasure hid in a field, and that of the one pearl of great price, and afterwards the close parallels between the parables of the tares and of the dragnet, with which the chapter closes. I do not pretend to certainty on these points, but have found so much light and help from the proposals of F.W. Grant, that I suggest that his interpretations be taken as the basis for the present study. This view will not carry universal assent, but will certainly merit the closest attention. On verses 44 to 46 his interpretation was that the treasure is Israel, while the pearl is the church.

If it is kept in mind that this series of seven parables represents the first comprehensive view afforded by Scripture of the long inter-Advent period, then any scribe wishing to be instructed into the Kingdom of heaven, and bearing in mind "the things old," would immediately enquire: "Where does the main subject of our Sacred Scriptures, our holy, chosen, beloved nation of Israel stand in these mysteries? The answer is in verse 44, and, in summary, is threefold. First, what was from the beginning Jehovah's treasure, is still so. Secondly, during all the period of these mysteries the treasure is hidden in the world. Thirdly, a Man, (surely no other than He Who has already been seen as the principal person in effective control of all, the Son of Man) is to pay the ransom price in order that the world, and with the world the treasure, might be his. Time will be well spent in a study of each of these three.

Since there has been in some quarters so strong an insistence that the family of God cannot be divided, but must be found in the end to be one, and not two, then the place occupied in Scripture by the entirely separate calling and destiny of Israel and the Church is worth examining in detail, so that witnesses of today might be added to the clear witness of brethren of former times on so important a matter. The reader's patience will only permit a limited selection of the extremely extensive Bible witness to the past, present and future of the nation of Israel as the Lord's earthly treasure. It is a pity that a selection must be so limited, since it is difficult to escape the suspicion that many who have been persuaded against this witness cannot have seriously read the Old Testament. Two quotations from Deuteronomy indicate that the undeniable separation of Israel by divine calling from the nations was not with a view to its having an ultimate destiny outside the nations, but that its earthly calling should in the end be seen to be at their head, as the channel of God's blessing to the whole world. Deuteronomy 32:8, "When the Most High divided to the nations their inheritance, when he separated the sons of Adam, he set the bounds of the people according to the number of the children of Israel". (Ibid. 28:12, 13) "The Lord shall open unto thee his good treasure, the heaven to give the rain unto thy land in his season, and to bless all the work of thy hand: and thou shalt lend unto many nations, and thou shalt not borrow. And the Lord shall make thee the head, and not the tail; and thou shalt be above only, and thou shalt not be beneath."

One quotation must suffice to illustrate that the relation which the divine lovingkindness from and at the beginning desired to maintain with His people was that Israel was **His "peculiar treasure"**. This appears in Exodus 19:5 as God's intention in the origination of Israel's nationhood at the Exodus: and again in the Deuteronomic review preparatory to their entry into Canaan. (Deuteronomy 14:2 and 26:18, 19) "The Lord hath avouched thee this day to be his peculiar people...and to make thee high above all nations which he hath made, in praise, and in name, and in honour." The word 'peculiar' has a quite distinct meaning: they were to be a treasure for His own possession and for none other. No believing heart can mistake that the heart of Jehovah was deeply involved in these transactions, and the Old Testament language through to the end intensifies this divine longing. Listen to Jeremiah 2:2 and sense the love and longing of God reaching back over the centuries and witnessing so certainly that His heart has not changed towards them. "Thus saith the Lord; I remember thee, the kindness of thy youth, the love of thine espousals, when thou wentest after me in the wilderness." Of all the Old Testament books the Psalms give the most lively evidence of the lovingkindness and tender mercy of the Lord which was the joy and rejoicing of His people in their joyful worship. "Nevertheless my lovingkindness will I not take away utterly from him, nor suffer my faithfulness to fail. My covenant will I not break, nor alter the thing that is gone out of my lips." In the light of this tenor of Old Testament Scriptures, few will doubt that the parable of the treasure is during this period, now so long protracted; the heart of the blessed God is still ever in remembrance of His own treasure, Israel.

The second lesson we have suggested from the parable is that during the whole period of these mysteries the treasure is hidden in the world. To promote the blessing of Israel in the sense of the fulfilment to them of Old Testament prophecy is no part of the activity of seeking the Kingdom during the present time. Perhaps we have to make the difficult effort to distinguish between Israel, the original whole nation to which the promises were made, and the small remnant centred on the Jews who returned from the Exile with Ezra. The distinction is not easy to maintain consistently since, for instance,

James includes them all in the Salutation of his epistle. If, however, we make the distinction, the meaning of the parable is sufficiently clear. The ten tribes which formed the kingdom of Israel under Jeroboam and his successors represented the mass of the nation. In B.C. 721 Samaria was taken by the Assyrian king, the inhabitants of the kingdom of Israel were deported, and the kingdom ceased to exist. From that day forward history knows nothing of them. In prophecy, however, they have a prominent place. They re-appear after the appearing of Christ, they are re-united with restored Judah, and with its ancient unity recreated under "great David's greater son," Israel is seen to be Jehovah's treasure. Where has this people existed through these centuries of oblivion? The parable answers the question. "The Kingdom of heaven is like unto treasure hid in a field." Jehovah's treasure has been hidden in the world. Its whereabouts is quite unknown, and by many its existence unsuspected.

Bible prophecy makes reference to the future restoration of the ten tribes in many places. After the future appearing of the "Son of Man coming in the clouds of heaven with power and great glory, (Matthew 24:30, 31) he shall send his angels with a great sound of a trumpet, and they shall gather together his elect from the four winds, from one end of heaven to the other." Who are these elect, to be assembled after the coming of Christ as King? Scripture answers the question quite specially. Isaiah 11 describes the establishment of the Kingdom in the Branch out of Jesse, and continues, "And it shall come to pass in that day, that the Lord shall set his hand again the second time to recover the remnant of his people, which shall be left, from Assyria, and from Egypt, and from Pathros, and from Cush, and from Elam, and from Shinar, and from Hamath, and from the islands of the sea. And he shall set up an ensign for the nations, and shall assemble the outcasts of Israel, and gather together the dispersed of Judah from the four corners of the earth. The envy also of Ephraim shall depart, and the adversaries of Judah shall be cut off: Ephraim shall not envy Judah, and Judah shall not vex Ephraim." (vv 10-13) Hosea also deals largely with Ephraim, and includes a promise, "For the children of Israel shall abide many days without a king, and without a prince, and without a sacrifice, and without an image, and without an ephod, and without teraphim: afterward shall the children of Israel return, and seek the Lord their God, and David their king; and shall fear the Lord and his goodness in the latter days." (Hosea 3:4,5) The elect to be gathered after the appearing of Christ are therefore unquestionably the ten tribes of Israel, to be joined to Judah, and the Israel which was Jehovah's treasure will by these events be recreated. The end of the story — "so bright with love, so dark with woe" — of Israel as the treasure for the heart of the Lord, shines like the rainbow after rain. "For a small moment have I forsaken thee; but with great mercies will I gather thee. In a little wrath I hid my face from thee for a moment; but with everlasting kindness will I have mercy on thee, saith the Lord thy Redeemer...For the mountains shall depart, and the hills be removed; but my kindness shall not depart from thee." (Isaiah 54:7-10) "The Lord thy God in the midst of thee is mighty;...he will rejoice over thee with joy; he will rest in his love, he will joy over thee with singing." (Zephaniah 3:17)

The third element in our summary of the parable of the treasure is that the Son of Man has paid the ransom price (all that He had) so that the world, and with it the treasure, might be His own. The reference to the place called Calvary, and to the precious blood of Christ, is unmistakable. As the Person in effective control of the whole enterprise of the Kingdom, a number of actions are attributed to the Son of Man in these parables. From the beginning he sows the seed, and at the end He sends forth His angels. But no other action can rightly be set alongside this action, in which without any limit He pours out His all in sorrow and shame, in anguish and death, to secure the world for the sake of the treasure. That He has indeed bought the world is evidenced by the fact that even those who most horribly deny His claims (false teachers who bring in damnable heresies), are nevertheless bought by Him. (2 Peter 2:1)

And now we come to the parable of the pearl. "Again, the kingdom of heaven is like unto a merchant man, seeking goodly pearls: who, when he had found one pearl of great price, went and sold all that he had, and bought it." The first point of interest is that the Lord is presented, not as a diver, but as a merchant. He saw it, and His heart was set upon it, not in the darkness and slime of the ocean depths, but in the beauty with which all the daring and skill of the diver and the craftsman could endow it. It satisfied His heart, not in its original night of hideous gloom, but displayed with the loveliness which He Himself would impart to it. "A glorious church, not having spot, or wrinkle, or any such thing, but...holy and without blemish," was the object before Him when He loved it and gave Himself for it. It is most worthy of note that contained in the word 'gave' is the same abandon without limit which is represented by the phrase 'sold all that he had.' The word **paradidomi** means more than simply 'give', as the various English words used to translate it show very strikingly. It is translated 'betray' to describe the action of Judas Iscariot, for the action of the chief priests when they 'delivered' Him to Pontius Pilate, and when Pilate 'delivered' Jesus to be crucified. Exactly the same word occurs in Romans 8:32, "He that spared not his own Son, but delivered him up for us all," and in Galatians 2:20, "the Son of God, who loved me, and gave himself for me." Finally, it occurs in the passage which gave rise to this train of thought, Ephesians 5:25, "Christ loved the church, and delivered himself up for it." It clearly bears the meaning of delivering over without any withholding to the extremity of suffering and death. In the words of the parable, emphasis seems to be placed on there being **one** pearl of such great price: its unity is of importance. Although the stress is on the fact that among all the pearls seen by the merchant man, only this one possessed the qualities he was seeking for, this accentuation of its unity naturally draws attention to the unity which is an essential mark of the church. The "one flock" of John 10:16, ("there shall be one flock and one shepherd,") and the unity of the disciples in John 17:11, 21, 22, foreshadows the unity achieved in the church by the union of Jews and Gentiles who believe. The church is repeatedly stated to be essentially one, as the body of Christ.

In bringing to a close this consideration of the fifth and sixth of the seven parables of the chapter, we ought to recall that they are the first part of the three parables uttered in private to the disciples inside the house, in contrast with the first four spoken by the seaside to the great crowds gathered to hear Jesus. The first four present the outward form which the mysteries of the Kingdom present to the world, and answer the questions which sooner or later arise in the mind of every active disciple. Is it to be expected that so many hearers will fall away, and why do they do so? Why is so much error abroad? Why are the big battalions always on the side of the false? The last three parables reveal the secret of what there is in the Kingdom enterprise for the heart of the Lord, and since during the period covered by this chapter the situation regarding the treasure is static, this is especially true of the parable of the pearl. Here is the germ of what expands in the epistles to occupy a dominant position. At the first explicit mention of the church, with one tremendous flash of final and victorious revelation, the active powers of evil so prominent in Matthew thirteen and in experience, are relegated to defeat. "I will build my church; and the gates of hell shall not prevail against it." (Matthew 16:18) The attitude of the disciple seeking first the Kingdom of God will surely mirror that of the pious Israelite. "Pray for the peace of Jerusalem: they shall prosper that love thee." (Psalm 122:6) "If I forget thee, O Jerusalem, let my right hand forget her cunning ... if I prefer not Jerusalem above my chief joy." (Psalm 137: 5,6)

Finally, we have in these two parables in embryo the only references in the chapter to the Cross and its meaning. This central theme of all Scripture expands and deepens on page after page of the epistles, until it rings out in the song of the worshippers above. "Thou art worthy ... for thou wast slain, and hast redeemed us to God by thy blood out of every kindred, and tongue, and people, and nation." "Unto him that loved us, and washed us from our sins in his own blood ... to him be glory and dominion for ever and ever."

MATTHEW 13:47-50

47 Again, the kingdom of heaven is like unto a net, that was cast into the
48 sea, and gathered of every kind: Which, when it was full, they drew to shore, and sat down, and gathered the good into vessels, but cast the bad away.
49 So shall it be at the end of the world: the angels shall come
50 forth, and sever the wicked from among the just, And shall cast them into the furnace of fire: there shall be wailing and gnashing of teeth.

Chapter 12

THE NET CAST INTO THE SEA

We have already mentioned the obvious fact that this parable is, on the surface, closely parallel with that of the Tares. If they were intended by the Lord to describe in parallel the same preaching of the Word, then the existence of the parable of the Net, and its separation at the end of the sèries, would indeed be difficult to understand. Here again the proposals of F.W. Grant have been found so illuminating, that we shall take them as the basis of our explanation. In this last parable "we find, not another aspect of the divine dealings with the mingled crop in the field of Christendom, but a new acting, whether in grace or judgment, after the merchant man has possessed himself of his pearl, or in other words, after the saints of the past and present time are caught up to Christ." There are at least two good reasons for taking this view: the shortness of the operation of casting and drawing in the net, and the fact that Scripture undoubtedly describes a separate evangelisation belonging explicitly to the end of the age.

If we compare the parables of the Tares and the Net, we have to reckon with the fact that the Palestinian harvest was four or five months after the sowing time. It could very well be that the sowers and the reapers were different persons. In fact, in the parable they were different persons. In contrast with this, the whole action of the casting and drawing in of the net would cover only a few hours, and normally the same persons would carry out the whole operation. These facts, taken together with the relative positions of the two parables in the whole series, are consistent with the view that the parable of the Tares describes the preaching of the Word which was begun by the Lord, and is still continuing, while the parable of the Net reveals an evangelisation to be begun and completed at the end of the age.

The clearest prophecy of a gospel to be preached after the present preaching of the gospel of the grace of God is completed, is given by the Lord and recorded in Matthew 24:14. "This gospel of the kingdom shall be preached in all the world for a witness unto all nations; and then shall the end come." A closely related prophecy is found in Revelation 14:6; "And I saw another angel fly in the midst of heaven, having the everlasting gospel to preach unto them that dwell on the earth, and to every nation, and kindred, and tongue, and people." Remembering that in the parable the net is cast into the sea, it is also interesting to notice that in the previous chapter, (Revelation 13:1), the sea is symbolic of the mass of peoples, nations, and tongues out of which the first beast arises. Likewise in Luke 21:25, 26, ("the sea and the waves roaring; men's hearts failing them for fear"), the sea is again used as a symbol of the mass of mankind at the end of the age.

Having thus confirmed good reasons for accepting the parable of the Net as giving the first hint of the preaching of the gospel of the Kingdom at the end of the age, as the parable is found at the end of the series, reflection on it leads me to find the central interest in verse 48, which describes, in the parable as distinct from the interpretation in verse 49, the action of the fishermen dealing with the full net after drawing it to the shore. The centre of their interest was "the good." They gathered the good into vessels, and displayed little concern with the bad. The words employed indicate that they were bad in the sense of rotten or worthless, and that the good were so in the sense of beautiful or precious. It is this thought especially which explains the position of the parable grouped with those of the Treasure and the Pearl. The casting of the net produced and garnered something desirable and precious. In this third sphere of action also there is seen something precious in the sight of the Lord, and therefore of real concern to the scribe instructed into the Kingdom of heaven. As always, the explanation found in verse 49 goes beyond what is in the parable, and presents events outside the period of the Kingdom of heaven. When the time of the execution of judgment comes, the angels are occupied with the wicked, and they are cast into the furnace.

Before leaving the seven parables of Matthew 13, it will be helpful to review comprehensively what is given to the disciples inside the house, when contrasted with what is recounted to the crowds outside. This inside information includes, first, the interpretation of the parable of the Tares, in contrast with the parable itself, which follows the parable of the Sower. The discourse uttered 'within', then proceeds to the three parables of the Treasure, the Pearl and the Net. We note this superficially strange splitting of the **explanation** of the parable of the Tares from the parable itself, and the linking together of this explanation with the three parables of the beautiful and the precious. Very special importance and interest are seen to belong to the additional light the Lord's own disciples needed to understand the full meaning of the parable of the Tares. Its consequences, far beyond what could be seen by those living during the period of the Kingdom of heaven, are linked with the revelation of what was to be in all this for the heart of the Lord Himself by being given inside the house.

The parable of the Tares had ended (verse 30), with the tares gathered together into bundles ready for destruction, and the wheat hidden within the barn. This fairly clearly means the saints removed to heaven, and the field of Christendom containing only the evil to be destroyed. The explanation given inside the house (verse 37), resumes the story at this point and supplies a great deal of information which the disciples would require to enable them to understand how His Kingdom would be cleared of all that offends, and how the righteous will be manifested in glory. These events will take place after the Lord has risen up and put an end to the mixed condition of Christendom now seen by the world. In and through these events the Kingdom of heaven is seen to issue in the Kingdom of the Son of Man on earth and the Kingdom of the Father in heaven.

Perhaps the interpretation of the Tares is linked with the last three parables because the persons and the classes who will compose these future forms of the Kingdom are indicated in more detail in the last three parables. In 1 Corinthians 10:32 Scripture presents a threefold division of mankind during the present period: "the Jews, the Nations, and the Church of God." Surely there will be something for the Lord out of each of these three sections of the human race. The view of the parables given here supplies an answer to this. In the Treasure and the Pearl and the Precious (taken out of the sea of all nations after the pearl is removed), the Lord is exulting over the thought of the fulness and extent of the way "He shall see of the travail of his soul, and shall be satisfied."

MATTHEW 16:13-19

13 When Jesus came into the coasts of Caesarea Philippi, he asked his
14 disciples, saying, Whom do men say that I the Son of man am? And
they said, Some say that thou art John the Baptist: some, Elias; and
15 others, Jeremias, or one of the prophets. He saith unto them, But
16 whom say ye that I am? And Simon Peter answered and said, Thou art
17 the Christ, the Son of the living God. And Jesus answered and said unto
him, Blessed art thou, Simon Bar-jona: for flesh and blood hath not
18 revealed it unto thee, but my Father which is in heaven. And I say also
unto thee, That thou art Peter, and upon this rock I will build my
19 church; and the gates of hell shall not prevail against it. And I will give
unto thee the keys of the kingdom of heaven: and whatsoever thou
shalt bind on earth shall be bound in heaven: and whatsoever thou shalt
loose on earth shall be loosed in heaven.

Chapter 13

THE KINGDOM OF HEAVEN AND THE CHURCH

We owe to the Venerable Bede the story of how, in A.D.664 a Council was convened at Whitby in North Yorkshire to decide whether the kingdom of Northumbria should give allegiance to the Roman usages or to the Irish or Columban forms received from Iona. Colman, for the Irish forms, appealed to the authority of the apostle John, through that of Columba of Iona. Wilfrid, for the Roman usages, pleaded the authority of the apostle Peter. After lengthy disputation, Wilfrid quoted in support of the claims of the bishop of Rome, the saying of the Lord which we have in Matthew 16:18,19: "Thou art Peter, and upon this rock I will build my church; and the gates of hell shall not prevail against it. And I will give unto thee the keys of the kingdom of heaven".

"When Wilfrid had spoken thus, the king said, "Is it true, Colman, that these words were spoken to Peter by our Lord?" He answered, "It is true O king!" Then says he, "Can you show any such power given to your Columba?" Colman answered, "None." Then added the king, "Do you both agree that these words were principally directed to Peter, and that the keys of heaven were given to him by our Lord?" They both answered, "We do." Then the king concluded, "And I also say unto you, that he is the door-keeper, whom I will not contradict, but will, as far as I know and am able, in all things obey his decrees, lest, when I come to the gates of the kingdom of heaven, there should be none to open them, he being my adversary who is proved to have the keys."

The idea that entrance into heaven is the same thing as entrance into the Kingdom of heaven is too naive to be considered seriously, but the disciple seeking the Kingdom will still everywhere meet the claims of the See of Rome, even though less naively than in the story of Northumbria, and he ought therefore to be ready with an understanding of the passage now to be studied, Matthew 16: 13-19. Moreover, what is more important, in these verses there bursts into Scripture the first explicit reference to the Church, which is seen to be the treasured and guarded possession of Christ, and one of the principal themes of the New Testament.

What brings this passage within the range of our present study is that verses 18 and 19 immediately disclose a certain connection between the

Church and the Kingdom of heaven. It will be most important to try to determine as exactly as possible what that connection is.

These verses contain the first mention of the Kingdom of heaven since the parables of chapter 13. In spite of the absence of the phrase, the intervening chapters deal with themes bearing clearly on fulfilment of the mysteries declared in the parables. Prominent among these themes are (a) the development of Christ's rejection by the Jews, (b) His mighty works proclaiming His worthiness to reign, and (c) the inclusion of Gentiles in the blessing dispensed by Him.

Taking the verses in order, the first subject, (verses 13-16) is Peter's confession, and this is the foundation for the great things which follow. Three titles of the Lord are joined in these verses: the Son of Man, the Christ, and the Son of the living God. The sources of the first of these are Psalm 8:4-8 and Daniel 7:13, 14: the Son of Man, made a little lower than the angels for the suffering of death, and afterwards crowned with glory and honour, to be set over all the earth: also, in Daniel the glorious Person to whom a kingdom over all the earth will be given at His coming. It signifies, therefore, a real man; one who as such was to be rejected and suffer death; and yet will rule over all. In the Lord's question, therefore, He was presenting Himself in a character which in its rudimentary meaning would be accepted by all — a real man — but had overtones of present suffering but universal authority. The answer of the 'man in the street' demonstrated recognition of some authentication of the preaching of Jesus by God, but complete blindness regarding His true majesty. (The story of Manoah and his wife in Judges 13:6 and 22 illustrates the immense difference between the two. They were interested in receiving a communication from a man of God, but prostrated with alarm at the realization that they had seen God.) And then, in response to the question addressed directly to themselves, Peter made the great confession: "Thou art the Christ, the Son of the living God."

O Saviour Jesus, Thou art indeed the Christ, the Saviour of the world! Thou art indeed the long-promised destroyer of the devil, Son of Abraham, Son of David, and Fulfiller of all the promises! Thou art in truth the Anointed Prophet, Priest and King! The hearts of thy people are inditing a good matter when they speak of Thee. Thou art fairer than the children of men; grace is poured into Thy lips; therefore God has blessed Thee for ever.

O Saviour Jesus, Thou art indeed the Son of the living God! No man knoweth Thee, but the Father. Thou art the brightness of His glory! Thou art the perfect expression of His substance! Thou art one with Him as the fountain of the all-conquering vigour of life. Death has no dominion over Thee. The gates of death shall surely fall before Thee, and Thou shalt surely triumph over the last enemy. All honour and majesty, all love and devotion be Thine both now and evermore!

"And Jesus answered and said unto him, Blessed art thou, Simon Bar-jona: for flesh and blood hath not revealed it unto thee, but my Father which is in heaven." Only the revelation from the Father could bring about such a conviction and such a confession. And now there are seen to be two Persons active in confirming such blessing to Simon. The Father had revealed, and now Jesus acts in His own personal, divine authority: "And **I also** say unto thee, That thou art Peter, and upon this rock I will build my church."

What was the rock on which Christ was to build His Church? We are in the extremely happy position of being able to ask Peter this epoch-making question. Question: Whom did **you** understand, Peter, as the rock on which the Church was to be built? Answer: (1 Peter 2:3, 4) "If so be ye have tasted that the Lord is gracious. To whom coming, as unto a living stone, disallowed indeed of men, but chosen of God, and precious, ye also, as living stones, are built up a spiritual house". Peter further helps us by quoting a Scripture, Isaiah 28:16. "Behold I lay in Zion for a **foundation** a stone, a tried stone, a precious corner stone, a sure **foundation**". Without any shadow of doubt, therefore, the Rock on which the Church was to be built was Christ, just confessed by Simon as the Son of God. In the second sentence quoted from 1 Peter 2, the relative 'whom' has its antecedent in the first sentence, and it is clearly "the Lord". The Gracious Lord, the Living Stone laid in Zion, is the one great rock-foundation for Christ's Church, and Peter, by the change of name announced by the Master, was made to partake in the rock-character, as also are the saints addressed in 1 Peter 2:5.

In the parable of the one pearl of great price we found a hint of an object for the heart of Christ in connection with the Kingdom of heaven. This hint is taken up and amplified in these verses: "My Church". At this point this name first enters Holy Scripture, and in clear connection with the Kingdom of heaven, which is at this moment our principal subject, and we must now address ourselves to enquire into the connection between the two.

The distinct personal action of the Lord is stressed: "I also say" (verse 18); "I will build" (verse 18); "I will give" (verse 19). In the sense in which the Church is considered in this primary passage, it is the sphere of the personal action of Christ. On the other hand, while the Kingdom commission remains under the authority of Christ, it is given by Him to be the sphere of responsibility of Peter, and this in two parts, first, the power of the keys, and secondly the power of binding and loosing.

The Lord's commission concerning the keys finds clear illustration in the gospels. Consider His denunciation of the Pharisees in Matthew 23:13: "But woe unto you, scribes and Pharisees, hypocrites! for ye shut up the kingdom of heaven against men: for ye neither go in yourselves, neither suffer ye them that are entering to go in." A similar condemnation is found in Luke 11:52: "Woe unto you, lawyers! for ye have taken away the key of knowledge: ye entered not in yourselves, and them that were entering in ye hindered." Remembering that the power of the keys was committed to Peter personally and not anywhere repeated as applying to the other disciples, it is only possible to see in the choice by God of Peter for the first preaching of the gospel to the Gentiles (as well as separately to the Jews) the fulfilment of this particular commission, "the keys of the kingdom of heaven." And with this, something exclusively given to Peter, agrees his speech at the council at Jerusalem: "ye know that how a good while ago God made choice among us, that the Gentiles by my mouth should hear the word of the gospel, and believe."

In contrast with this, the power of binding and loosing is repeated to the other disciples collectively in the 18th chapter; "Whatsoever ye shall bind on earth shall be bound in heaven: and whatsoever ye shall loose on earth shall be loosed in heaven". (verse 18) The sphere of the binding and loosing is on earth, not in heaven; but to such binding on and for earth, the authority of heaven will assure its approval and support. Edersheim (Life and Times of Jesus the Messiah) gives an illuminating comment on the meaning of these functions. "In interpreting such a saying of Christ to Peter, our first enquiry must be, what it would convey to the person to whom the promise was addressed. And here we recall, that no terms were in more constant use in Rabbinic Canon-Law than those of 'binding' and 'loosing' ... ' to bind' in the sense of prohibiting, and ... 'to loose' in the sense of permitting ... But this expression is, both in Targumic and Talmudic diction, not merely the equivalent of permitting, but passes into that of remitting, or pardoning." We might readily find these interpretations in Scripture itself, but this simply makes the comment of Edersheim the more interesting. The apostles unquestionably exercised the right to declare what was permitted or prohibited, and we possess their decrees as the apostles of Christ in the New Testament. They also exercised the authority to remit sins or retain them **on earth**. This is seen in the cases of Ananias and Sapphira and the incestuous person in 1 Corinthians 5.

The new light this passage sheds, therefore, on our subject, which is the Kingdom, is that during the absence of the Lord in heaven, the Kingdom of heaven is administered by men. In that aspect of the Church, therefore, which comes before us in this passage, that is, in the aspect according to which it is assured of victory, perhaps, in a sense it is even assured of infallibility, then it is exclusively the work of Christ. In the sense in which the Kingdom of heaven is under human administration, it is assured of the support of heaven, but not of infallibility. This becomes clear if we examine the rest of the New Testament, as we have already done, to establish the meaning of these commissions and promises.

There are two dominant views of the Church in the later New Testament. One continues the aspect presented by the Lord in Matthew 16. We must surely take it as the primary one, that in which the Lord's heart will be satisfied, and His will secured. There is infallibility here, for all depends immediately on Christ Himself, and His own 'I will'. Perhaps this view is found in 1 Peter 2:5 and Ephesians generally. But, for example, in 1 Corinthians 3:12-17 we have a very different view in which human administration is something for which abundant support is available, but all is to be tested, and much will be found to have come short. I quote an interesting comment by F.B. Hole: "In this great pronouncement the Lord spoke of His Church as being His own handiwork, against which all adverse wisdom and power could not prevail. What is done in the power of Divine life nothing can touch. Other Scriptures speak of the Church as the community professing allegiance to Christ, brought into being through the labours of those who take the place of servants of God. On that community failure was stamped from the outset, and it merges into the kingdom of heaven, of which we learn so much in chapter 13, and which the Lord mentions in verse 19 of our chapter. The keys of that kingdom were given to Peter — not the keys of the Church."

The succinct conclusion of the matter is therefore that there are two broad ways in which the church is viewed: one according to which it is assured of final triumph, and one when it is seen to be permeated by failure from the beginning — a mixed condition in which individual faithfulness will always have its reward. It is quite unjustified to apply the unconditional assurances given to the first, as though applicable to the second. In the first, victory depends entirely on Christ's person and work. In the second, any measure of victory is the result of individual fidelity, in which, alas, there is only too evident failure. The Church in the former sense — My Church, He calls it — will in all the beauty assured for it by the work of Christ be raptured to meet Him at His coming. After this, what remains of the Church as it depends on human responsibility will be spued out of His mouth. The Church in this sense appears to merge with the Kingdom of heaven since both are seen to be administered by failing men, and both contain the admixture of evil.

One final word regarding the claims of the papacy: its basic claim rests on an interpretation of Matthew 16:18 and 19 which is absolutely untenable. Furthermore, there is no trace afterwards in the New Testament of any primacy of Peter after his use of the keys. Only consider Acts 15 and the position of Peter at the council, or reflect dispassionately on his epistles, and any idea of such primacy simply vanishes away. Even if such primacy had ever existed, why should it be considered transmissible to the bishops of Rome? That Peter ever was at Rome rests on nothing stronger than tradition, and if he were, he could not have been its bishop in the sense that the pope is bishop of Rome, for no such concept of bishopric exists in Scripture, or existed at all for many years after Peter's death. Our faith rests on Christ and His word. Upon the rock of Peter's confession of Himself as the Son of the living God, made outside and prior to the Church, He is building His Church, and the gates of hell shall not prevail against it.

It might be desirable to add a few words more precisely on the persons involved. In the case of both, the Kingdom and the Church can and do on occasions include what is mere profession, as has just been explained. For this reason we cannot distinguish those included in the Church from those included in the Kingdom on the basis that either does or does not in all circumstances include mere profession. It is more appropriate in this connection to consider the persons who have real faith in Christ, and then it is apparent that the persons included in the Church and in the Kingdom must be identical. So long as the Church is on earth the obedience of faith is the only qualification for a real and true place in each.

When the Church shall be removed to heaven, then the Kingdom in visible power will be set up, and henceforward the persons composing the Kingdom and the Church will be distinct. It might be held that the members of the Church, as "the righteous shining forth in the kingdom of their Father", are still in the Kingdom, but the members of the Kingdom on earth are not members of the Church. If we return for a moment to the present time, although we have seen that the persons composing the Church and the Kingdom must be identical, this does not mean that the Church and the Kingdom are identical. The persons composing a family and a business may be identical, but the family and the business are not the same thing. The two entities will have different constitutions, different privileges and different responsibilities. The Kingdom and the Church are indeed very distinct. The Kingdom consists of everything that depends on the fact that here on earth we are subject to Christ as Lord. The Church consists of everything that springs from the fact that we are eternally one with Christ in heaven by the Holy Ghost sent down.

MATTHEW 16:28 to 17:8

28 Verily I say unto you, There be some standing here, which shall not taste of death, till they see the Son of Man coming in his kingdom.
1 And after six days Jesus taketh Peter, James, and John his
2 brother, and bringeth them up into an high mountain apart, And was transfigured before them: and his face did shine as the sun, and his
3 raiment was white as the light. And, behold, there appeared unto them
4 Moses and Elias talking with him. Then answered Peter, and said unto Jesus, Lord, it is good for us to be here: if thou wilt, let us make here three tabernacles; one for thee, and one for Moses, and one for Elias.
5 While he yet spake, behold, a bright cloud overshadowed them: and behold a voice out of the cloud, which said, This is my beloved Son, in
6 whom I am well pleased; hear ye him. And when the disciples heard it,
7 they fell on their face, and were sore afraid. And Jesus came and touched
8 them, and said, Arise, and be not afraid. And when they had lifted up their eyes, they saw no man, save Jesus only.

MATTHEW 18:4 and 21-35

4 Whosoever therefore shall humble himself as this little child, the same is greatest in the kingdom of heaven.
21 Then came Peter to him, and said, Lord, how oft shall my brother
22 sin against me, and I forgive him? till seven times? Jesus saith unto him, I say not unto thee, Until seven times: but, Until seventy times seven.
23 Therefore is the kingdom of heaven likened unto a certain king,
24 which would take account of his servants. And when he had begun to reckon, one was brought unto him, which owed him ten thousand
25 talents. But forasmuch as he had not to pay, his lord commanded him to be sold, and his wife, and children, and all that he had, and payment
26 to be made. The servant therefore fell down, and worshipped him,
27 saying, Lord, have patience with me, and I will pay thee all. Then the lord of that servant was moved with compassion, and loosed him, and
28 forgave him the debt. But the same servant went out, and found one of his fellow-servants, which owed him an hundred pence; and he laid hands on him, and took him by the throat, saying, Pay me that thou
29 owest. And his fellow-servant fell down at his feet, and besought him,
30 saying, Have patience with me, and I will pay thee all. And he would
31 not: but went and cast him into prison, till he should pay the debt. So when his fellow-servants saw what was done, they were very sorry, and
32 came and told unto their lord all that was done. Then his lord, after that he had called him, said unto him, O thou wicked servant, I forgave
33 thee all that debt, because thou desiredst me: Shouldest not thou also have had compassion on thy fellow-servant, even as I had pity on thee?
34 And his lord was wroth, and delivered him to the tormentors, till he
35 should pay all that was due unto him. So likewise shall my heavenly

Father do also unto you, if ye from your hearts forgive not every one his brother their trespasses.

MATTHEW 19:23

23 Then said Jesus unto his disciples, Verily I say unto you, That a rich man shall hardly enter into the kingdom of heaven.

MATTHEW 20:1-16

1 For the kingdom of heaven is like unto a man that is an householder, which went out early in the morning to hire labourers into his vineyard.
2 And when he had agreed with the labourers for a penny a day, he sent
3 them into his vineyard. And he went out about the third hour, and saw
4 others standing idle in the marketplace, And said unto them; Go ye also into the vineyard, and whatever is right I will give you. And they went
5 their way. Again he went out about the sixth and ninth hour, and did
6 likewise. And about the eleventh hour he went out, and found others standing idle, and saith unto them, Why stand ye here all the day idle?
7 They say unto him, Because no man hath hired us. He saith unto them, Go ye also into the vineyard; and whatsoever is right, that shall ye
8 receive. So when even was come, the lord of the vineyard saith unto his steward, Call the labourers, and give them their hire, beginning from the
9 last unto the first. And when they came that were hired about the
10 eleventh hour, they received every man a penny. But when the first came, they supposed that they should have received more; and they
11 likewise received every man a penny. And when they had received it,
12 they murmured against the goodman of the house, Saying, These last have wrought but one hour, and thou hast made them equal unto us,
13 which have borne the burden and heat of the day. But he answered one of them, and said, Friend, I do thee no wrong: didst not thou agree
14 with me for a penny? Take that thine is, and go thy way: I will give
15 unto this last, even as unto thee. Is it not lawful for me to do what I
16 will with mine own? Is thine eye evil, because I am good? So the last shall be first, and the first last: for many be called, but few chosen.

Chapter 14

THE TRANSFIGURATION

Let us put v.8 in the forefront of our meditation on this great chapter. After their sleep was past, they lifted up their eyes and "saw no man save Jesus only." Our prayer as we move forward can ever be fixed on these two words, "Jesus only".

What was the purpose and character of the Transfiguration? In what particular character does it present to us our Saviour, the Son of God? The story follows immediately on that of the previous chapter. It was the fulfilment of the promise given in Matthew 16:28, that is, six or eight days previously: "They shall see the Son of Man coming in his kingdom". To this closely agree the other Synoptic Gospels. They will have seen "the kingdom of God come with power". (Mark 9:1). "They see the kingdom of God". (Luke 9:27). Thus the Transfiguration was, in its true purpose and meaning for the disciples, a sight of Him in the glory of His coming Kingdom. It seems natural to us to think of the Transfiguration as the shining out of the divine glory of the One who had veiled that glory in flesh. But we must be subject to the Word itself in this as in all other things. Some will find this view inconsistent with the words from out of the cloud, "This is my beloved Son, in whom I am well pleased." This would be a mistake, for that most excellent name of Son is used in Scripture not only of Christ's eternal sonship in deity, (the only begotten of the Father), but also as a title of the Messiah in manhood and beginning in time. In Psalm 2, to the king anointed on Zion's holy hill, Jehovah addresses Himself thus: "Thou art my Son; this day have I begotten thee. Ask of me, and I shall give thee the heathen for thine inheritance, and the uttermost parts of the earth for thy possession." Also, in Isaiah 42 Jehovah sings of His delight in His King: "Behold my servant,...mine elect, in whom my soul delighteth; ...he shall bring forth judgment to the Gentiles...and the isles shall wait for his law." The Sonship of the Lord Jesus in manhood and in time is most clearly witnessed in Luke 1, when the angel, after promising that the Holy Ghost would come upon Mary and that the power of the Highest would overshadow her, continues "therefore also that holy thing which shall be born of thee shall be called the Son of God."

Just as we have seen that Peter explains in his first Epistle the true meaning of the Rock, so in his second Epistle he looks back to the

Transfiguration. After speaking in 1:11 of the Kingdom of our Lord and Saviour Jesus Christ, he proceeds in v.16 "For we have not followed cunningly devised fables, when we made known unto you the power and coming of our Lord Jesus Christ, but were eyewitnesses of his majesty. For he received from God the Father honour and glory, when there came such a voice to him from the excellent glory, This is my beloved Son, in whom I am well pleased. And this voice which came from heaven we heard, when we were with him in the holy mount. We have thus the word of prophecy made surer (New Translation); whereunto ye do well that ye take heed, as unto a light that shineth in a dark place, until the day dawn, and the day star arise in your hearts." In other words it was the word of prophecy about the coming Kingdom of our Lord Jesus Christ which was made surer to him when they saw this vision of His majesty on the holy mount.

Standing unique in the splendour of His majesty, the Son of God is the central figure in this most brilliant scene. It was to remind them of the honour uniquely due to Him alone that the disciples were left in the end seeing "no man, save Jesus only." But this sample of the coming Kingdom required the presence of two men with Jesus in the glory, as well as the disciples on the ground. Moses and Elijah were respectively the men who had instituted and restored the true religion of Israel, and this is not the only hint that the Old Testament saints will share the heavenly glory of the Kingdom. But probably they are here principally in virtue of the facts that one, Moses, had died, and is found here in the glory after his death. The other, Elijah, did not die, but was taken to heaven with the chariots of the Lord. They are thus fitting representatives of the saints who die, (like Moses), and will be raised from the dead so as to be with the Lord when He comes in His Kingdom, and also of those other Church saints who, (like Elijah), will not die, but will pass into the presence of the Lord alive at His coming. The disciples on the ground represent God's earthly people, Israel, having their part in the Kingdom on earth. There is little wonder that Peter gives so important a place to this vision. Perhaps more than all the words of the Lord this vision made real for them the splendour and certainty of that Kingdom.

What was the effect intended by the Lord in the subsequent lives of the disciples? Immediately after the great confession in Matthew 16:16, Jesus began to show His disciples how that "he must...suffer...and be killed, and be raised again the third day." It must have been a staggering shock to them to learn that following Him was not to lead immediately to their entrance with Him into His Kingdom, and that there would be an intermediate period of suffering and rejection. And this is true for all who will follow the Master from that time to this. "If any man will come after me, let him deny himself, and take up his cross, and follow me. For whosoever will save his life shall lose it: and whosoever will lose his life for my sake shall find it." (vv.24,25) The disciples had not bargained for this. What could possibly keep and give them strength to cope with an experience such as that on which they were now to enter? Many mercies are given to comfort and strengthen the disciples, but at this point the need was met by this vision of Christ in His Kingdom glory. If there is a deep, dark valley to pass, how different if a bright shining land of glory is visible ahead.

Through the gospel page and Peter's letter the mountain top experience is made available to every disciple, but it was to three chosen men that this vision was first given. With a wisdom and love far beyond our understanding the Lord prepares His servants individually for what in His plan lies ahead of them. Theirs was to be an outstanding responsibility in the Church's earliest days. James was an early martyr; and Peter and John were manifestly pillars on whom much depended. It was the choice of the Lord Himself which matched their future responsibility with the special nearness to Himself given them in the holy mount, at the raising of Jairus's daughter, and in Gethsemane. To see what they saw, the appropriate place is "an high mountain apart." Eyes which are to see clearly the things of God have to be lifted above the plain of man's busy activities, and this is witnessed in the several mountain scenes of Scripture.

It is in Luke's Gospel that we read of the occupation of those who were with the Lord in the glorious majesty of His Kingdom. If we only had Matthew's account, when we read that Moses and Elias were talking with Jesus, we might well have enquired what could possibly be the subject of such a conversation. We read in Luke 9: 31 that they were talking about His exodus, of His going out of the world by way of the cross, concerning which He had just been speaking to the disciples. They were speaking together about His death which was about to be accomplished at Jerusalem, and indeed the cross of Christ and the precious blood of the Lamb slain will for evermore be the theme occupying those who are with Him in His Kingdom.

Peter made the mistake of trying to put on an equality with Himself the two men who were His companions in the vision, and therefore the bright cloud overshadowed them. And indeed there were dark clouds lying ahead, clouds of deepest blackness for the Lord Himself and for those who would be His own. They had been given this vision so that amidst the darkest clouds they might ever be fortified by the knowledge that they will be with the Saviour in the glory to follow. And out of that overshadowing cloud there came the words, "This is my beloved Son, in whom I am well pleased; hear Him." Of all the themes on which we might meditate, none is more wonderful, and, when all is said and done, more effective within us, than the knowledge that the Father's full delight is centred in the Son.

Shortly after the story of the Transfiguration in Matthew's Gospel, there follow some significant additions to what has already been discussed in the Sermon on the Mount on the subject of the character appropriate to the Kingdom society. The opening section of chapter 18 contains the lessons the Lord drew from the sight of the little child set by Him among the disciples. Their question was "Who is the greatest in the kingdom of heaven?" The first lesson is a character application, and it is crystallised in v.4. "Whosoever therefore shall humble himself as this little child, the same is greatest in the kingdom of heaven." In classical Greek literature humility is usually despised as slavish, grovelling and mean. It is a great and characteristic quality of Bible teaching that it dethrones the heathen virtue of high-mindedness, and sets up humility as a central virtue of the Christian character. In the poetical books of the Bible, especially in the Old Testament idiom, the contrasts between successive lines are often very illuminating. Two such cases come to mind. Luke 1:52: "He hath put down the mighty from their seats, and exalted them of low degree". Proverbs 29:23: "A man's pride will bring him low: but honour shall uphold the humble in spirit".

High thoughts of self, that is, pride, is the opposite of humility. Two outstanding patterns of humility are the Lord Himself, and this little child. "Being in the form of God...He emptied himself...being found in fashion as a man he humbled himself". In the latter of these two sentences, He is His people's Teacher and Example. "Learn of me, for I am meek and lowly in heart." Here in Matthew 18:4, the pattern is the little child set in the midst. The humility of a little child is especially appealing. It is the un-selfconscious lowliness, dependence and absence of pretension which marks little children which confers greatness in the Kingdom society. The citizens of this all-conquering Kingdom bear the badge of humility. The second lesson drawn by the Lord from this little child, points us to the determination not to cause to stumble "one of these little ones who believe in me."

In the same chapter, vv.23 to 25 the lesson of forgiveness is vividly portrayed in the parable in which the Kingdom of heaven is likened to two debtors, one owing ten thousand talents and the other a hundred denarii. The first, on pleading for mercy, is freely forgiven the debt. The second, who owed to the first servant one hundred denarii, is resolutely refused forgiveness. The fellowservants do not fail to perceive the wretchedness of such behaviour. The duty, for disciples, of mutual forgiveness, in this case unconditionally, could never have more incisive demonstration than in this parable. It is a fruitless exercise to attempt to determine the equivalents of these two debts in any modern currency; what matters is the ratio between the two, and this is easy to calculate. In terms of the silver currency of New Testament times, 10,000 talents was equal in value to six hundred thousand times 100 denarii; the ratio is equal to that of ten miles to one inch. The parable is saying, in terms readily understood by the hearers, You have been forgiven a ten mile debt: is it conceivable that you can hesitate to forgive your fellow-servant his one inch debt? No command of our Saviour is more consistently ignored than the unconditional duty of mutual forgiveness; and nothing would be more effective in the Kingdom society than the habit of simple obedience to this command.

In the next chapter, (19:23, 24), the Lord gives His comment on the defection of the rich young ruler. "Verily I say unto you, That a rich man shall with difficulty enter into the kingdom of heaven...It is easier for a camel to go through the eye of a needle, than for a rich man to enter into the kingdom of God." I can find no justification for the often-expressed idea that the eye of a needle was a figure of speech representing a small pedestrian entry through a city wall, through which, when other gates were closed, a camel might, by dint of much pushing and pulling, be urged with extreme difficulty. It seems rather to mean what it says, that for a rich man to enter the Kingdom is impossible to nature. It is, many may thank God, not impossible for the grace of God. Here is surely another reminder of the stark contrast, and indeed reversal of the values of any known merely human society, (in which there are few doors which cannot be unlocked by money), in the society of the Kingdom of God.

If one looks back on these three parts of the moral values which belong to the Kingdom society, it becomes manifest that explanation alone will not avail to cause the evil weeds of pride, an unforgiving spirit, and the love of money, so natural to the soil of our hearts, to wither away. Explanation can and does stimulate the renewed mind by a vision of the good, but set seasons of devotional meditation or reflection in the secret place with the Lord will be required and will be effective in giving place for the Spirit of God to write Christ on our hearts. Through such means alone can the will be stimulated to action.

The parable of the labourers in the vineyard (Matthew 20:1-16), introduced as another likeness of the Kingdom of heaven, is generally admitted to be amongst the most difficult to interpret with confidence, yet we must seek help from God to understand it aright. The context is the rewards in the Kingdom of the Son of Man awaiting those who have forsaken all and followed Jesus (19:27-29). It illustrates the two sayings: "many that are first shall be last; and the last shall be first", (19:30), and "the last shall be first, and the first last". (20:16). The words 'first' and 'last' recur in vv. 8, 10, 12, and 14. The last were those hired at the eleventh hour and the first those hired early in the morning. The first were dis-satisfied and regarded the rewards as unjust. The householder replied that the payments were based on his goodness and no-one had suffered injustice. If we suppose that the penny was a superlatively magnanimous payment for a day's work, (and there is nothing to decide otherwise), then the parable is a reminder that rewards in the Kingdom are measured by grace and not limited to justice. To this view we shall return in our last chapter.

The two parables mentioning the Kingdom which appear in Matthew 21:33-43, (the wicked husbandmen), and 22:(1-14), (the marriage of the king's son), are mutually supporting in their dispensational references to the Jews' treatment of God's Son. The wicked husbandmen represented the chief priests and Pharisees who did not yield fruit to God and finally killed His Son. As a result of this appalling rejection, the Kingdom was to be given to the disciples and their successors. The murderers in the second of these parables represent also the Pharisees, who refused the invitation to honour the Son and murdered the messengers. Therefore they were destroyed and their city burned, and the Gospel invitation went out to outsiders of both Jews and Gentiles. It was in immediate consequence of this rejection of Himself and His message by the Jewish leaders that, after the terrific invective against these leaders of Matthew 23, the Lord, discoursing on the destruction of the temple, occupies His disciples with the future of the Kingdom in the great discourse to which we now turn.

MATTHEW 24:1-31

1 And Jesus went out, and departed from the temple: and his disciples
2 came to him for to shew him the buildings of the temple. And Jesus said unto them, See ye not all these things? verily I say unto you, There shall not be left here one stone upon another, that shall not be thrown
3 down. And as he sat upon the mount of Olives, the disciples came unto him privately, saying, Tell us, when shall these things be? and what shall
4 be the sign of thy coming, and of the end of the world? And Jesus
5 answered and said unto them, Take heed that no man deceive you. For many shall come in my name, saying, I am Christ; and shall deceive
6 many. And ye shall hear of wars and rumours of wars: see that ye be not troubled: for all these things must come to pass, but the end is not
7 yet. For nation shall rise against nation, and kingdom against kingdom: and there shall be famines, and pestilences, and earthquakes, in divers
8, 9 places. All these are the beginning of sorrows. Then shall they deliver you up to be afflicted, and shall kill you: and ye shall be hated of all
10 nations for my name's sake. And then shall many be offended, and shall
11 betray one another, and shall hate one another. And many false
12 prophets shall arise, and shall deceive many. And because iniquity shall
13 abound, the love of many shall wax cold. But he that shall endure unto
14 the end, the same shall be saved. And this gospel of the kingdom shall be preached in all the world for a witness unto all nations; and then
15 shall the end come. When ye therefore shall see the abomination of desolation, spoken of by Daniel the prophet, stand in the holy place,
16 (whoso readeth, let him understand:) Then let them which be in Judaea
21 flee into the mountains:...For then shall be great tribulation, such as was not since the beginning of the world to this time, no, nor ever shall
22 be. And except those days should be shortened, there should no flesh
27 be saved: but for the elect's sake those days shall be shortened.... For as the lightning cometh out of the east, and shineth even unto the west; so
28 shall also the coming of the Son of man be. For wheresoever the carcase is, there will the eagles be gathered together.
29 Immediately after the tribulation of those days shall the sun be darkened, and the moon shall not give her light, and the stars shall fall
30 from heaven, and the powers of the heavens shall be shaken: And then shall appear the sign of the Son of man in heaven: and then shall all the tribes of the earth mourn, and they shall see the Son of man coming in
31 the clouds of heaven with power and great glory. And he shall send his angels with a great sound of a trumpet, and they shall gather together his elect from the four winds, from one end of heaven to the other.

MATTHEW 25:1-13

1 Then shall the kingdom of heaven be likened unto ten virgins, which

2 took their lamps, and went forth to meet the bridegroom. And five of
3 them were wise, and five were foolish. They that were foolish took
4 their lamps, and took no oil with them: But the wise took oil in their
5 vessels with their lamps. While the bridegroom tarried, they all
6 slumbered and slept. And at midnight there was a cry made, Behold,
7 the bridegroom cometh; go ye out to meet him. Then all those virgins
8 arose, and trimmed their lamps. And the foolish said unto the wise,
9 Give us of your oil; for our lamps are gone out. But the wise answered,
saying, Not so; lest there be not enough for us and you: but go ye
10 rather to them that sell, and buy for yourselves. And while they went
to buy, the bridegroom came; and they that were ready went in with
11 him to the marriage: and the door was shut. Afterward came also the
12 other virgins, saying, Lord, Lord, open to us. But he answered and said,
13 Verily I say unto you, I know you not. Watch therefore, for ye know
neither the day nor the hour wherein the Son of man cometh.

MATTHEW 25:31-46

31 When the Son of man shall come in his glory, and all the holy angels
32 with him, then shall he sit upon the throne of his glory: And before
him shall be gathered all nations: and he shall separate them one from
33 another, as a shepherd divideth his sheep from the goats: And he shall
34 set the sheep on his right hand, but the goats on the left. Then shall the
King say unto them on his right hand, Come, ye blessed of my Father,
inherit the kingdom prepared for you from the foundation of the
35 world: For I was an hungred, and ye gave me meat: I was thirsty, and
36 ye gave me drink: I was a stranger, and ye took me in: Naked, and ye
clothed me: I was sick, and ye visited me: I was in prison, and ye came
37 unto me. Then shall the righteous answer him, saying, Lord, when saw
we thee an hungred, and fed thee? or thirsty, and gave thee drink?
38 When saw we thee a stranger, and took thee in? or naked, and clothed
39,40 thee? Or when saw we thee sick, or in prison, and came unto thee? And
the King shall answer and say unto them, Verily I say unto you,
Inasmuch as ye have done it unto one of the least of these my brethren,
41 ye have done it unto me. Then shall he say also unto them on the left
hand, Depart from me, ye cursed, into everlasting fire, prepared for the
42 devil and his angels: For I was an hungred, and ye gave me no meat: I
43 was thirsty, and ye gave me no drink: I was a stranger, and ye took me
not in: naked, and ye clothed me not: sick, and in prison, and ye visited
44 me not. Then shall they also answer him, saying, Lord, when saw we
the an hungred, or athirst, or a stranger, or naked, or sick, or in prison,
45 and did not minister unto thee? Then shall he answer them, saying,
Verily I say unto you, Inasmuch as ye did it not to one of the least of
46 these, ye did it not to me. And these shall go away into everlasting
punishment: but the righteous into life eternal.

Chapter 15

THE OLIVET DISCOURSE

The Olivet Discourse occupies the twenty-fourth and twenty-fifth chapters of Matthew's Gospel, and deals with the future of the Kingdom in relation to the Second Coming of Christ. The direct references to the Kingdom are:— 24:14, the Second Coming will be preceded by the preaching of the gospel of the Kingdom in all the world: the Second Coming is described in terms closely allied to the prophecy in Daniel 2 from which we have derived the expression 'Kingdom of God': in Matthew 25:1 the parable of the ten virgins is declared to be a similitude of the Kingdom of heaven: and in 25:34 and 40, when the Son of Man gathers all nations before Him, He will be the King, and the blessed will inherit the Kingdom. The Discourse is in three parts. The first, 24:1-44, deals with the Jews and Jerusalem. The third, 25:31-46, concerns the Gentile nations, and plainly resumes at the point where the first broke off. Between the two there are three parables having their application to Christ's disciples in the intervening period. Thus, once again, we see the interests of the Lord set out with relevance to the Jews, the Nations, and the Church of God, and are reminded that this framework for viewing events is the one dictated by God's word in many instances. It is therefore the framework we should adopt.

Jerusalem and the Jews. Matthew 24:1-44 perhaps more than any other Scripture requires the reader to keep in mind the apostolic injunction, "rightly dividing the word of truth". It was for me dark and full of discord and difficulty until I learned that it deals with salvation, not as it is known by the believer today, but as it will come to the believing remnant of Jews in Jerusalem at the end of the age. Seen thus, it is one of the most useful frameworks of prophetic truth to be found in Scripture.

A careful reader of Matthew's Gospel will have already received a hint from 10:5-23 that when the Son of Man comes again there will be found Jewish disciples in the cities of Judah occupying the same relationship with Himself as at His first coming. In that chapter, sending out the twelve disciples to preach the Kingdom, and warning them of hostility and betrayal, the Lord concludes, "Ye shall not have gone over the cities of Judah till the Son of Man be come." This is quite in line with many Old Testament

Scriptures, in which the Church period is simply ignored and the story of the end of the age told as if it were continuous with the past.

Viewed in this light, the story of Matthew 24:4-39 may be parpahrased in the following manner. Jewish disciples of Jesus, faithful to Him in His absence amid a generally hostile Jewish nation in Jerusalem, which is under a Roman tyrant, shall be subjected to all kinds of trials: deception by false Christs; wars and rumours of wars; famines, pestilences and earthquakes; intense persecution; treachery, deception and defection from among themselves. Their watchword was to be 'hold out', because salvation depends on endurance through these beginnings of sorrows to the end. The reason they must hold out is that the gospel of the Kingdom must be preached throughout the world: then the end comes. At the moment they see an idol set up in the temple, (a plain sign known to the faithful from the book of Daniel), their outlook changes, and the watchword is to be instant flight to the mountains outside Judaea. Then there shall be a great tribulation, so severe that if it were not shortened for the elect's sake, the human race would be exterminated. The tribulation will be accompanied by intensified deception by false Christs and by miracles. At the end there will be a breakdown of all government, and all mankind shall see the Son of Man coming in the clouds of heaven with great glory. He shall gather the elect from all the earth. Throughout this time there will be continued eating, drinking, marrying and giving in marriage until the judgment of the coming Christ falls.

The whole sequence of events outlined in the previous paragraph **must** be subsequent to the rapture of the Church to meet Christ in the air. If not, the two passages, (Matthew 24:5-41 and 1 Thessalonians 4:15-18) would be in flat contradiction.

It will be interesting to attempt a similar interpretation, in paraphrase and summary, of Daniel's visions. The ancient Roman Empire will become divided into ten kingdoms. At the end of the age, there will arise among these a new empire, world-wide and cruel. Its ruler will be a blasphemer of God and a persecutor of His saints. He will make a seven-year treaty with the mass of the Jews, but will break it after three and a half years. Thereafter he will abolish the Jewish worship, and substitute an idol placed in the temple. He will persecute the faithful, and this will be a time of unprecedented trouble for the Jews. After a reign of a further three and a half years, (the remainder of the seven), he will be destroyed by Christ at His coming in the clouds of heaven with glory. Christ shall then set up a Kingdom which shall never give place to another, and His saints shall share His Kingdom with Him.

Reflection on these two accounts of the end of the age, both coming from God, will make it clear that they are telling the same story — in Daniel from the point of view of the external events of world history — in Matthew from the standpoint of Jewish disciples living through it, and able to read these very words, and to derive the fullest measure of strength and comfort from the Lord's assurances.

"Behold the Bridegroom". The three parables of the middle section of the Discourse are, first, the faithful and evil household servants; second, the wise and foolish virgins; and third, the faithful and wicked servants of the absent master; (respectively 24:45-51, 25:1-13, 25:14-30). The lesson, from these three standpoints, is watchfulness, wakefulness, and diligence during the Lord's absence. The matter is in each case adjudged on the Master's arrival. For the moment we shall consider in particular the parable of the virgins, which, in common with so much that has come before us in Matthew's Gospel, is explicitly described as a likeness of the Kingdom of heaven.

The central event of this parable is the cry in v. 6, "Behold the Bridegroom!" Since we have ten virgins, including five who were wise, we have not here an explicit representation of the one Church, the bride of Christ, but the teaching given is edging towards this truth, which is so prominent in the Epistle to the Ephesians. The character stamped upon the story is that of the Bridegroom and the joy of the marriage feast. The parable presents four stages. First, a company takes up the position of going out to meet Christ. This company bears three important marks of the Church. They are separated from the world – they went forth. They are light-bearers – they witness during the night. Their destiny is ostensibly to enter in with Christ. But all are not what they appear. They pass for being true until the test comes. At the second stage, they **all** went to sleep. That is, as for the meeting for which they had gone out at first, they lost sight and sense of it. At the third stage there arises the midnight cry, "Behold the Bridegroom!", accompanied by the call to take up again the original position, going out to meet him. The fourth and final stage is presented in v. 10, "the Bridegroom came".

Within the limits of the parabolic method, the intent is clear. The parable broadly sketches certain features of the course of events between the first 'going out' of the Christian profession, and the moment when Christ, the Bridegroom, comes. Let us attempt to seize the main message. That Christians everywhere lost sight and sense of the promise of His coming is only too sadly true to history. After the Bible days little was heard of the personal expectation of meeting Christ at His coming until long after the Reformation. This is one vital element in which its works were not found perfect before God. The reformers, under God, uncovered the truth of justification by faith, for which we shall ever thank God. But they did not uncover the personal hope of meeting Jesus at His coming. One of the most widely known and loved of the songs of Christ, the beloved, the Bridegroom, is that of Samuel Rutherford, as interpreted by Mrs Cousins in her hymn, "the bride eyes not her garment, but her dear bridegroom's face". But even so long after the Reformation, the eye of his faith was explicitly fixed on his going to Christ by his imminent death, and not on meeting Him at His coming. Up to this time and long beyond it, "they all slumbered and slept." A Critical Theology sees the fact that the personal expectation of meeting Christ at His coming was given up, and offers an explanation: Christians found that they had been mistaken in ever expecting it. The word of Jesus in this parable foresees that the hope would be given up, and gives the true explanation: they all went to sleep. The event will prove that Critical Theology is in error: they were not mistaken in expecting it. Jesus will certainly come again as His word has promised; and He always intended that every generation should live in expectation of His coming. Around this personal hope the Christian's dearest affections cluster, and from this hope he receives the most effective of his stimuli to faithful endurance and service.

Without any question the midnight cry arose in the early years of the last century. Since that time, and not before it, hundreds of thousands of Christians in every land have been rejoicing in this personal hope of the Saviour's coming. The exact form of the cry is to call attention to His Person: "Behold the Bridegroom!" It is part of the great universal theme of Scripture: "Ecce Homo", "Behold the Man"; "Behold my servant...in whom my soul delighteth", cries Jehovah in Old Testament prophecy. "Behold the Lamb of God" calls the voice of one crying in the wilderness at His first coming. "Behold the man!", said Pilate, as He went forth to Calvary. "Behold me standing at the door", pleads the Lord to the churches. And the glorious sight will indeed "gladden each waiting, watchful eye".

The detail of vv. 8-12 perhaps present a difficulty. When the midnight cry is heard, the unwise, seeing their lamps going out, first attempt to obtain oil from the wise. While they are away buying for themselves, the door is shut, and they find they have forfeited entry altogether. This might be taken as teaching that mere professors are finally shut out from the moment of the cry, that from that moment it is too late to do anything about it, too late to obtain oil, too late to receive the Holy Ghost so as to be ready for His coming. In fact we know that it is the closing of the door which closes opportunity of salvation, and the details making up the outward form of the parable at this point surely teach, first, that from the beginning some were never really ready for the Bridegroom's coming: and second, that receiving the Holy Spirit must be a directly personal matter between each individual and the Lord.

The parable is obviously addressed to the disciples and not to the unconverted, and the message is contained in v.13. All those virgins went to sleep. They were wrong to go to sleep, and the Lord is grieved about it. v.13 seems to say, Do not do as they did. Do not go to sleep in the matter of personal expectation of meeting the Bridegroom at His coming. Keep awake, therefore, for ye know neither the day nor the hour wherein the Son of Man cometh. That 'watch' essentially means 'keep awake' is shown by the opposites in such a passage as 1 Thessalonians 5:10, where the same word is employed: "Whether we wake or sleep". These virgins were wrong to go to sleep, and both for the disciples at the beginning and for ourselves between the midnight cry and the coming of the Bridegroom, the appeal is, Do not be like those virgins. Do not go to sleep in the matter of personal expectation of meeting the Bridegroom at His coming. In the presence of this appeal from the Lord, we feel ourselves near to a flash of understanding of the Song of songs 5:2, "I slept, but then my heart awakened: it is the voice of my beloved that knocketh, saying, Open to me...my love...for my head is filled with dew, and my locks with drops of the night".

"The bridegroom came". This is the event which lies before us, how near we do not know. "They that were ready went in with him to the marriage." The prospect of the joy of the marriage feast, so often a theme of Scripture, is calculated to keep the disciple awake in joyful expectation. And the closing of the door on all those whose faith is mere appearance, is the end of the day of salvation.

The Sheep and the Goats. The opening words of this prophecy clearly establish the time referred to. It is subsequent to the fulfilment of 24:30, when the Son of Man shall come with glory. 24:31 also mentions His angels, and here in 25:31 all His holy angels are with Him. As we have already noted, the events leading up to this Advent are subsequent to the Rapture of the saints to meet the Lord in the air. From this point in time so clearly marked, this prophecy proceeds with new detail. Then, "he shall sit upon the throne of his glory", and all the Gentile nations shall be gathered before him for judgment. There is no reason to doubt that this means the **living** nations. Thus the Olivet Discourse completely disposes of all the world. The Jews and Israel have already found their destiny at His coming. The saints of the interval between the comings have entered in and the door is shut. The judgment here described extends the actual reign of the Son of Man to the uttermost limits of earth. All nations not already dealt with are here, and for this reason the short passage in which the Lord describes the session separating the nations one from another as a shepherd separates his sheep from the goats is portentous in the extreme. The criterion by which the individuals composing the nations will be judged is most clearly postulated. They are sheep or goats, on the right hand or on the left, blessed or cursed, passing to the Kingdom prepared or to the fire prepared, according to how they have received the King's brethren. Since they will have been received in all the world subsequent to the Rapture, they are certainly His Jewish messengers by whom the gospel of the Kingdom will have been preached in all the world. This is the final judgment for all living. The judgment of the dead is described in Revelation 20:12.

We shall take time only to look more closely at the teaching of this passage about the Kingdom. In the first place, this is one of the rare places in which the Lord is called the King. It is no longer the time of the mystery

Kingdom, possibly no longer the Kingdom of heaven. The time of consummation has come, and the King is personally present on the throne of His glory. Also, in v. 34 is a very interesting description of the Kingdom then present. It is "the kingdom prepared for you from the foundation of the world." Let us compare this time scale with three other Scriptures: "for thou lovedst me before the foundation of the world", (John 17:24): "the precious blood of Christ, as of a lamb without blemish and without spot: who verily was foreordained before the foundation of the world", (1 Peter 1:19,20): and "he hath chosen us in him before the foundation of the world," (Ephesians 1:4). Our passage is, by contrast, in exactly the same terms as Matthew 13:35, relating to the parables of the Kingdom, "things which have been kept secret from the foundation of the world". Thus the Kingdom is to be distinguished on a time scale from certain other actions and events. This distinction is quite simple and unequivocal. The Kingdom belongs to earth and its history, that is, its planning dates **from** the foundation of the world, and this means when the work of creation was completed. (Hebrews 4:3). The actions and events which date from **before** the foundation of the world are (1) the Father's love for the Son, (2) the fore-ordaining of Christ's sacrifice, and (3) the election of the Church. These latter are the subjects of eternal counsel; the Kingdom belongs to earth and time.

Finally there is something for the heart of every disciple in the King's verdict: "Inasmuch as ye have done it unto one of the least of these my brethren, ye have done it unto me." During the period of His absence, what can we do which is personally for Him and pleasing to Him? (Is not this laying up treasure in heaven?) We can show to His brethren the care and love we would wish to show to Himself. His brethren here are His Jewish brethren, evidently in keenest suffering and reproach, wanderers, naked, sick or in prison. This is how the nations will treat the messengers of the Kingdom. In principle, however, is it possible not to apply these most moving words of the Saviour to every opportunity of ministering to His own people at any moment?

1 CORINTHIANS 15:20-28

20 But now is Christ risen from the dead, and become the firstfruits of
21 them that slept. For since by man came death, by man came also the
22 resurrection of the dead. For as in Adam all die, even so in Christ shall
23 all be made alive. But every man in his own order: Christ the firstfruits;
24 afterward they that are Christ's at his coming. Then cometh the end, when he shall have delivered up the kingdom to God, even the Father;
25 when he shall have put down all rule and all authority and power. For
26 he must reign, till he hath put all enemies under his feet. The last
27 enemy that shall be destroyed is death. For he hath put all things under his feet. But when he saith all things are put under him, it is
28 manifest that he is excepted, which did put all things under him. And when all things shall be subdued unto him, then shall the Son also himself be subject unto him that put all things under him, that God may be all in all.

2 THESSALONIANS 1:4-7

4 ...your patience and faith in all your persecutions and tribulations that
5 ye endure: Which is a manifest token of the righteous judgment of God, that ye may be counted worthy of the kingdom of God, for which ye
6 also suffer: Seeing it is a righteous thing with God to recompense
7 tribulation to them that trouble you; And to you who are troubled rest with us, when the Lord Jesus shall be revealed from heaven with his mighty angels...

1 THESSALONIANS 2:12

12 That ye would walk worthy of God, who hath called you unto his kingdom and glory.

COLOSSIANS 4:11

11 These only are my fellowworkers unto the kingdom of God.

1 CORINTHIANS 15:50

50 Now this I say, brethren, that flesh and blood cannot inherit the kingdom of God; neither doth corruption inherit incorruption.

1 CORINTHIANS 6:9-11

9 Know ye not that the unrighteous shall not inherit the kingdom of God? Be not deceived: neither fornicators, nor idolaters, nor adulterers,
10 nor effeminate, nor abusers of themselves with mankind, Nor thieves, nor covetous, nor drunkards, nor revilers, nor extortioners, shall inherit
11 the kingdom of God. And such were some of you: but ye are washed, but ye are sanctified, but ye are justified in the name of the Lord Jesus, and by the Spirit of our God.

GALATIANS 5:19-23

19 Now the works of the flesh are manifest, which are these; Adultery,
20 fornication, uncleanness, lasciviousness, Idolatry, witchcraft, hatred,
21 variance, emulations, wrath, strife, seditions, heresies, Envyings, murders, drunkenness, revellings, and such like: of the which I tell you before, as I have also told you in time past, that they which do such
22 things shall not inherit the kingdom of God. But the fruit of the Spirit
23 is love, joy, peace, longsuffering, gentleness, goodness, faith, Meekness, temperance.

1 CORINTHIANS 4:20

20 For the kingdom of God is not in word, but in power.

ROMANS 14:17

17 For the kingdom of God is not meat and drink; but righteousness, and peace, and joy in the Holy Ghost.

Chapter 16

THE KINGDOM IN THE EPISTLES

In Paul's epistles the writer assumes that his readers know about the Kingdom of God. Its existence and meaning underly his teaching and instruction. Particularly is it clear that his readers knew already that there is a present form of the Kingdom, and yet the Kingdom in its power remains to be present in a future dispensation. The future form will be in power and glory, while the present form consists in personal and individual allegiance to God in Christ.

One section has laid its spell on students of Scripture both ancient and modern, because of what it says about the subjection of the Son to the Father. In 1 Corinthians 15:24-28 we shall for our present purpose concentrate on its remarkable teaching on the Kingdom. The paragraph uses three points in time as its scale of reference. First, the resurrection of Christ. "Now is Christ risen from the dead." (v.20). Secondly, the resurrection of His saints at His coming. "Afterward they that are Christ's at His coming." (v.23) Thirdly, the end, when death is destroyed. (vv.24-26) If we had been entirely dependent on this passage, who would have thought that two thousand years were to intervene between the resurrection of Christ and His second coming? Yet so it has been already. It is evident that the "he must reign" of v. 25 comes between the resurrection of His saints and "the end". During this interval Christ will possess the Kingdom, and at its close He will deliver it up to God because its purpose will have been accomplished, that is, to put down all authority and power and to destroy every enemy. The exact agreement of all this with Revelation 20 is very evident. There we have prophesied the first resurrection, (v.5); the thousand years' reign of Christ with His saints, (v.4), and the end, when death and hell are destroyed. The only additional knowledge supplied in the Revelation is the exact duration of the reign, a thousand years.

2 Thessalonians 1:5 is noteworthy, not only for its comfort for Christians of every time and place in "persecutions and tribulations", as well as its stimulus to "patience and faith", but also for its doctrine about the Kingdom. The prospect set before them is "rest with us" (says Paul). Such rest is to be realised in the Kingdom of God, and the Kingdom of God awaits the revelation of the Lord Jesus from heaven attended by His mighty angels in

the future day of vengeance.

For the remainder of the allusions to the Kingdom of God in Paul's epistles, let us think of them in the framework suggested in Chapter 2: first, those containing the phrase, "unto the kingdom of God"; second, those including the phrase, "inherit the kingdom of God"; and third, those beginning, "the kingdom of God is...". It will prove helpful to consider the first as presenting actions and events which will have results in the future Kingdom of God; the second as stressing the character and behaviour which mark out those who are sure to enter on their inheritance in the future Kingdom of God; and the third as portraying the nature and essential being of the present Kingdom.

To the Thessalonians, recently converted, Paul writes that God "hath called you unto his kingdom and glory". The context is dealing with the conversion of the saints addressed, how they had "turned to God from idols, to serve the living and true God; and to wait for his Son from heaven". The agency had been the Word in Holy Ghost power, the gospel, and it is already implied that such a call and destiny demanded a certain standard of behaviour — "to walk worthy". The addition of "and glory" proves that the future Kingdom is meant, the Kingdom as it is to be established when Jesus comes in glory with all His holy angels. Paul also writes that workers with him in the gospel field were working towards the establishment of that Kingdom. "These only are my fellow-workers unto the kingdom of God." By analogy with the previous quotation, this probably also means the future Kingdom, but it may also include the present form.

The next class of citations include the word 'inherit', and this is at a first approach defined in 1 Corinthians 15:50, "flesh and blood cannot inherit the kingdom of God". Inheriting the Kingdom of God cannot take place in this life: that is to say, it cannot come about before "the dead shall be raised...and we shall be changed". This statement gives the basic clue to understanding the passages using this phrase. Somewhat earlier in 1 Corinthians (6:9-11) we have a most instructive passage on this theme. "Know ye not that the unrighteous shall not inherit the kingdom of God? Be not deceived: neither fornicators, nor idolaters, nor adulterers, nor effeminate, nor abusers of themselves with mankind, nor thieves, nor covetous, nor drunkards, nor revilers, nor extortioners, shall inherit the kingdom of God. And such were some of you: but ye are washed, but ye are sanctified, but ye are justified in the name of the Lord Jesus, and by the Spirit of our God". The context here is going to law with fellow-Christians. v.1. contrasts going to law before the unrighteous and before the saints. The latter will judge the world; "we shall judge angels". The individuals at fault not only went to law, but they themselves defrauded others and so became unrighteous. Such people shall not, says the apostle, 'inherit the kingdom', that is, shall not enter into possession by right, of the exercise of divine authority in governing the world. Thus, clearly, what is envisaged is a time when God by His saints administers

His Kingdom. Such is the meaning of the Kingdom of God, and of inheriting in it, in the setting of this passage. It should have been a basal axiom, well-known to Christians, that persons of such characters and behaviour will never inherit the Kingdom of God, and this becomes an earnest appeal to Christian believers not to be such people. Here is the firmest possible stand against Christians taking on the behaviour of a permissive society around them. The characters and actions of vv. 9 and 10 provide a description of Corinthian society, notorious in Bible times, in the classical age of Greece, and long before. It is the more remarkable that we have preserved in Holy Scripture relating to Corinth a standard of Christian behaviour and discipline applicable in every time and place. There is no excuse for either laxity or despair when we are confronted by a society as permissive as that of Corinth, the byword of dissipation and corruption of manners. Some of the very people addressed had been formerly numbered amongst the ranks enumerated, but now they were washed, sanctified and justified in the Name of the Lord Jesus and by God's Spirit. The burden of 1 Corinthians 6:9-11 is repeated in Ephesians 5:5.

How is so immense a change in behaviour to be effected, and how maintained? The answer is suggested by the last phrase of the quotation from 1 Corinthians 6:11; "by the Spirit of our God". This is the answer and the burden of Galatians 5:31. After listing the foul progeny of the flesh, the passage continues, repeating former warnings, "they which do such things shall not inherit the kingdom of God". In this case the positive watchword of victory has already been disclosed : "walk in the Spirit, and ye shall not fulfil the lust of the flesh". What is the flesh? And is it still alive in the believer indwelt by the Spirit of God? The flesh is that portion of my spiritual being where sin dwells, and which is not subject to the law of God, nor indeed can be. The flesh is still very much alive in the believer, though he is indwelt by the Holy Spirit. The matter is explained at length in Romans 7 and 8, and by this concept of the flesh in Galatians 5:19-21, Paul's underlying appeal to the Kingdom of God is integrated with the general basis of his moral teaching, centred on the cross and the Spirit. For this reason Galatians 5:21 is a most important part of our study of the Kingdom of God. An outline of this moral teaching might run somewhat as follows. Romans 7:15-23 is the record of a most interesting and important introspection, the observations made, and the conclusions drawn. The writer, using the first person, records that on looking within himself, he observes an 'I' which delights in the law of God, but that this 'I' is not in control of the 'I' that acts in his behaviour. Reasoning by the Spirit on these empirical facts, he concludes that it is no more 'I' which does wrong but indwelling sin. The home of indwelling sin is the flesh. The two notes of victory are that God has condemned sin-in-the-flesh through the cross, and that He has given His Spirit to dwell within each believer, and to be the dominant power.

In Galatians 5, once the characters and actions which will prevent a man's inheriting the Kingdom of God are unmasked and identified as the works of the flesh, then the parallel truth is brought forward that love, joy, peace, longsuffering, gentleness, goodness, faith, meekness, and temperance are the fruit of the Spirit. The works of the flesh are to come under the cross, in order that when the believer walks in the Spirit, this lovely fruit may be seen. This triumphant conclusion is a hint of a truth at which we shall soon arrive, that the Kingdom of God is righteousness, peace, and joy in the Holy Ghost.

This leads us to the third class of Pauline references to the Kingdom of God, those which, by including the phrase "the kingdom of God is...", give instruction on the nature of the Kingdom. The first of these to which we refer is again in 1 Corinthians (4:20). "For the kingdom of God is not in word, but in power." At this point, once again there flashes out an appeal to a known fundamental truth, that where the ministry which is Christ's service is concerned, there is the Kingdom of God, and therefore there is power. The meaning of this appeal is not in doubt. The opponents of Paul and of his message at Corinth thought they could flout him. He was in their eyes a spectacle to the world, a fool for Christ's sake; weak and despised, labouring, reviled, persecuted; his bodily presence was weak, and his speech contemptible. They were mistaken in seeing only this view. His ministry did not concern the world, to which their estimate belonged. It concerned the Kingdom of God, and the Kingdom of God is in **power**. He was able to come to them with a rod. He could deliver a man to the power of Satan for the destruction of the flesh. The things he wrote are the commandments of the Lord. The weapons of his warfare were mighty through God to the pulling down of strongholds, casting down imaginations and every high thing that exalted itself against the knowledge of God, and bringing into captivity every thought to the obedience of Christ. In these phrases, 'the commandments of the Lord', 'the obedience of Christ', is the very essential being of the Kingdom of God, and therefore there is power with it, the power of God.

In Romans 14:17 we have what is perhaps the most frequently quoted of these Pauline references to the Kingdom of God. "The kingdom of God is not meat and drink; but righteousness, and peace, and joy in the Holy Ghost." These words occur in the context of some who tended to give high priority to their right to eat and drink certain things, to the harm and stumbling of other believers. There is the distinction between the 'weak' (v.1 and ch. 15:1), and the 'strong', (ch. 15:1), and Paul identifies himself with the latter. But there were snares for the strong as well as for the weak. The snare for the weak is to judge the other. The tendency of the strong is to despise the other. Both are corrected in 14:3, "Let not him that eateth despise...Let not him that eateth not condemn". It is the former, despising, which is in the end the burden of the apostle's message. "If thy brother be grieved with thy meat, now walkest thou not charitably." The matter is brought to the touchstone of love, but also to another criterion equally fundamental, the authority of God, the lordship of Christ, as embodied in the Kingdom of God. The Kingdom of God is the acknowledged framework within which the lives of true disciples unfold themselves. To adduce its nature is the last word. The Kingdom of God does **not** consist in eating and drinking. This is the negative. The disciple must eat and drink so long as he is flesh and blood. And his eating and drinking come under the authority of God. But the essential being of the Kingdom of God as already established in the hearts of men and women by the Word is not in such externals as eating and drinking. The essential nature of the Kingdom is within, in the realm of spiritual qualities and realities, righteousness, peace and joy. Action is indeed controlled by Kingdom allegiance, but actions which are in themselves neutral, such as eating and drinking, are to be appraised by whether they spring from, or issue in, righteousness, peace, and joy in the Holy Ghost.

At this point there appears to be a close connection between the present and future forms of the Kingdom. The Old Testament prophets deal very fully with righteousness, peace, and joy in the Messianic Kingdom. What they say, therefore, will cast light on Romans 14:17 which we are now considering. Descriptions of the future earthly Kingdom of God stressing these qualities are particularly frequent in the Psalms and in Isaiah. Psalms 96 to 99 are amongst those which celebrate the time when it shall be said, "The Lord reigneth". Look at vv. 10 to 13 of Psalm 96. When the Lord reigns, He will judge the people with righteousness, and on this score the heavens and the earth, the fields and the trees of the wood enter into joy and gladness. In Psalm 98, because He has shown His righteousness, therefore the hearer is called to make a joyful noise, to rejoice and sing praise. In Psalm 72 the mountains shall bring peace to the people because of righteousness: and in the days of the great King the righteous shall flourish and abundance of peace so long as the moon endures. In several parts of Isaiah there occur hymns in praise of Messiah's Kingdom, and in almost every case these three qualities are prominent. Chapters 25 to 27 form one such extended passage. In that day, the righteous nation shall enter in, and there is the promise, "Thou wilt keep him in perfect peace, whose mind is stayed on thee; because he trusteth in thee". The inhabitants of the earth shall learn righteousness, and the Lord will ordain peace. Look also at ch. 32. When a King shall reign in righteousness, then "the work of righteousness shall be peace, and the effect of righteousness, quietness and assurance for ever. And my people shall dwell in a peaceable habitation, and in sure dwellings and quiet resting places". When the Lord shall have filled Zion with judgment and righteousness, then "the wilderness and the solitary place shall be glad, and the desert shall rejoice, and blossom as the rose," and rejoice with joy and singing. "The ransomed of the Lord shall return, and come to Zion with songs and everlasting joy upon their heads: they shall obtain joy and gladness, and sorrow and sighing shall flee away". At the end of Isaiah, (ch. 66), the heaven is called on to rejoice with Jerusalem, to be glad with her, and rejoice with joy, "for thus saith the Lord,

Behold, I will extend peace to her like a river".

Two observations spring to mind on reflecting on these lyrical descriptions of the future Kingdom. There is joy because there is peace, and there is peace because there is righteousness. This is in perfect accord with the way of joy and peace in the early part of Romans. "Therefore being made righteous by faith, we have peace with God...and rejoice in hope of the glory of God". A second observation is that these blessings are made available to the people of God because they are in God. God's righteousness is a theme of Scripture from the beginning. God's peace is promised to those who pray. The righteousness and peace which lead to true joy are rooted in the being of God and of Christ. And therefore, when God rules, these things are the very essence and nature of such a Kingdom. Eating and drinking, and all other neutral actions fall into place when the authority of God and of Christ are at the deepest level acknowledged, accepted, and acted on. God's righteousness is available to faith through the blood of Christ; and once that righteousness is known by faith, the believer has all joy and peace in believing.

We are thus returning in these thoughts to the point made earlier, that when the believer obeys Christ in all the details of life and service, (and that is the Kingdom of God), then such obedience links him with all that is in God. All the breadth and length, and depth and height of all that is in God's heart and towards which He is working is immediately available by and in the acceptance of God's authority, that is, in God's Kingdom.

LUKE 19:11-27

11 And as they heard these things, he added and spake a parable, because he was nigh to Jerusalem, and because they thought that the kingdom
12 of God should immediately appear. He said therefore, A certain nobleman went into a far country to receive for himself a kingdom,
13 and to return. And he called his ten servants, and delivered them ten
14 pounds, and said unto them, Occupy till I come. But his citizens hated him, and sent a message after him, saying, We will not have this
15 man to reign over us. And it came to pass, that when he was returned, having received the kingdom, then he commanded these servants to be called unto him, to whom he had given the money, that he might know
16 how much every man had gained by trading. Then came the first,
17 saying, Lord, thy pound hath gained ten pounds. And he said unto him, Well, thou good servant: because thou hast been faithful in a very
18 little, have thou authority over ten cities. And the second came, saying,
19 Lord, thy pound hath gained five pounds. And he said likewise to him,
20 Be thou also over five cities. And another came, saying, Lord, behold,
21 here is thy pound, which I have kept laid up in a napkin: For I feared thee, because thou art an austere man: thou takest up that thou layedst
22 not down, and reapest that thou didst not sow. And he saith unto him, Out of thine own mouth will I judge thee, thou wicked servant. Thou knewest that I was an austere man, taking up that I laid not down, and
23 reaping that I did not sow: Wherefore then gavest not thou my money into the bank, that at my coming I might have required mine own with
24 usury? And he said unto them that stood by, Take from him the pound,
25 and give it to him that hath ten pounds. (And they said unto him,
26 Lord, he hath ten pounds.) For I say unto you, That unto every one which hath shall be given; and from him that hath not, even that he
27 hath shall be taken away from him, But those mine enemies, which would not that I should reign over them, bring hither, and slay them before me.

Chapter 17

"OCCUPY TILL I COME"

About thirty years before the Saviour illustrated His teaching with the parable of the pounds, (Luke 19:11 to 27), a deputation of leading Jews came from Judaea to Rome to seek an interview with Augustus. The occasion was a journey taken by Archelaus on the death of Herod, to petition Augustus for Herod's title of King of the Jews. The Jews had seen enough of Herodean rule to wish at all costs to put an end to it. So far as Herod the Great was concerned, his whole career was crimson with the blood of murder, which extended even to the strangulation of his favourite wife, Mariamne, the the only human being he passionately loved. As his life drew to its close every dark and brutal instinct of his character seemed to acquire fresh intensity, and he ordered the death of all the children under two years old in the environs of Bethlehem. The wail of anguish which arose from the mothers robbed of their infants, "Rachel weeping for her children", could not be hushed. Shortly after this frightful crime, the wretched old man lay in a savage frenzy awaiting his last hour. Knowing that no-one would shed tears for him, he determined that tears would be shed at his departure, and he had the principal families of the kingdom driven into the hippodrome, to be massacred at the moment of his death. Herod had named his son Archelaus as ruler after him. It is small wonder that when Archelaus went to Rome "to receive his kingdom, and return", that his citizens sent a message to Rome, saying, "We will not have this man to reign over us."

In the parable's meaning, by immeasurable contrast, it is the Lord Jesus, the true nobleman, who, after His death and resurrection, has gone into the far country of heaven to receive a kingdom and to return. No reader of these lines took his place amongst those who crucified the Lord of glory, but our lives send a message after Jesus every day. What is that message? Is it "Thine we are, thou son of David, and on thy side", or is it, "We will not have this man to reign over us"?

"A certain nobleman" is the subject of the parable, and there is an immense contrast between the low-born tyrants who occupied the thrones of the Herods, and Jesus, "King most wonderful". We can most completely agree with R.C. Trench: here "the epithet 'nobleman' has its highest fitness; for who was of such noble birth as He who, even according to the flesh, came of earth's first blood – was the Son of Abraham, the Son of David; also besides all this, was the eternal and only-begotten Son of God?" In the negative sense, (v.22), an utterly false knowledge of the nobleman, as a kind of Herod-character, was a disincentive to serving him wisely and faithfully. By implication, a true knowledge of him was the foundation motive for the good and faithful service of the other two servants mentioned. The entirely mistaken impression of his character was that he was an "austere" and grasping master; a strict, severe, and harsh person to account to. The good and faithful servants were so habituated to his presence and company that they knew him differently. The slothful and wicked servant had no experience of his company to awaken his heart, and his knowledge was ignorance. For the disciple seeking the Kingdom, it must be clear that there is no substitute for devotional habituation to the company of Jesus.

Passing in thought over those parts of Scripture which present to us the true character of the One who is away in heaven waiting to receive His Kingdom, there is no sweeter song than that of the prophet Isaiah on the subject of Jehovah's Servant in Isaiah 42, 49, 50 and 53. Isaiah 42:2 to 4 delineates His character in a series of negatives:

> v.2. "He shall not cry, nor lift up, nor cause his voice to be heard in the street."
> v.3. "A bruised reed shall he not break and the smoking flax shall he not quench."
> v.4. "He shall not fail nor be discouraged".

The meaning of v.2 is illuminated, not only by its quotation in Matthew 12:19, but also, we may be sure, by Paul's directions for servants in 2 Timothy 2:24. "The servant of the Lord must not strive; but be gentle, unto all men." The screaming, hysterical tone was not heard from this Servant, and is not to be heard from His servants. In the spirit of gentleness and aptness to teach, the servant of Christ is to conduct himself after the pattern of his Master in His service, with the prayerful expectation that God will intervene and grant repentance to opponents of the faith. "A bruised reed shall he not break and the smoking flax shall he not quench". Here is an endearing feature of the Servant. His is a task which demands the utmost tenacity of purpose and opponents in millions are to be overcome before His Kingdom is secured: but He does not, and will not ride roughshod over the feeble in order to bring it about. True it is that the lofty looks of man shall be brought low in that day, but it is also true that He will not break the bruised reed nor quench the smoking flax. "A smoking flax" – there is a point at which one touch can extinguish a smouldering wick, or gentle care may rekindle the flame. There is one point at which the temper of a touch means everything. The Servant of the Lord does not quench the smoking flax. How often do we feel like the smoking flax — a lamp with its flame expiring, due to our own folly or the cruelty of others? Surely Simon Peter was a smoking flax when, having denied the Lord with curses, he went out and wept bitterly. The Master did not quench the smoking flax. Deep and fervent prayer He had already made in intercession for Peter that his faith might not fail, that the flame dimly burning might not go out: a **look** at the critical moment, and finally, strong tender **words** restored the failing Peter to his purpose to serve the Lord.

"He shall not fail nor be discouraged, till he have set judgment in the earth". At this point in Isaiah, A.V. obscures one of the gems of the passage. To be in line with the words employed and translated in v.3, v.4 would read, "He shall not burn dim, or be crushed, until he have set judgment in the earth". The two words translated in v.3 "**smoking** flax" and "**bruised** reed" are the words used of the Servant Himself in v.4. He shall never burn low or dim. There is here the most charming contrast between this Servant and all the Herods of this world. On the stage of world history, the man of iron will and determination, of ruthless directness in attaining his goal, has usually done so at the expense of the feeble who stood in his way. The man who is himself utterly dependable is often unsympathetic to the weak. Often the only persons sympathetic to the feeble are those who are themselves feeble. Our Saviour is perfect: perfect in His love and wisdom in restoring our souls, in speaking a word in season to the weary, in giving power to the faint: but perfect also in that He is the everlasting God, Creator of the ends of the earth, who faints not, neither is weary. He shall never fail until His Kingdom be won.

Such is the true Nobleman. To know Him is to love Him. To love Him is to serve Him.

"And he called his ten servants, and delivered them ten pounds." (v.13) There is a very instructive comparison to be made at this point between the parable of the Kingdom of God in Luke 19 and that of the Kingdom of heaven in Matthew 25: 14-30. In the latter, three servants are mentioned, and "unto one he gave five talents, to another two, and to another one; to every man according to his several ability." In Matthew's parable, the servants are differently endowed, each in proportion to his ability. In Luke, each person equally receives one pound. It is clear that both parables present truth, but each presents a different facet of the truth about the endowment by the Lord of His servants for His work. The distinct views are doubtless in accordance with the individual purpose of each evangelist. Taking Matthew first, it is essential to distinguish between (a) each man's several and natural ability, and (b) the talents given him as something distinct and additional. The latter are in proportion to the former. In considering the service of the Lord, we easily ignore these facts. The natural endowment of ability is important, and is the result of God's forming vessels for His service. He formed Moses by his inherited ability, and by his training in the court of Egypt. It is nonsense to think that Moses had to undo the training he had received in Egypt. His confidence in it and in himself was wrong, and had to be surrendered, but Moses, trained in all the wisdom of Egypt, was the vessel formed by God for His use when thoroughly weaned from his confidence in himself in meek consecration to God. In like manner God formed Paul with his innate ability and by his schooling at the feet of Gamaliel. The opposite error is to forget that such natural ability is useless to God, without the washing of regeneration, the charismatic gift of the Spirit, and the purgation by which "vessels meet for the Master's use" are produced. The Lord can and does discipline and teach His servants in order to remove all confidence in the flesh, and to root their service in true knowledge of Himself and in dependence on His Spirit. In Luke's parable each of the ten servants receives in equal amount the capital required for trading. This draws attention to the equality of the servants as servants, and to the sense in which all are equally endowed. Examples of this equal endowment, (not, alas, often attended by equal diligence in their use), are the immeasurably great gift of the indwelling Spirit and the possession of the Word. In the availability to them of these superlatively effective endowments, all the Lord's servants are equal, and these gifts are unquestionably sufficient for the fulfilment of "every man his work".

And now, in v.13 we come to the verse I have chosen to be the closing message of this study of the Kingdom of God : "Occupy till I come."

Occupy. This word means 'employ in trading', and the object of the verb is the pound which each servant had received. An explanatory paraphrase might read, "Take this pound and employ it in trading until I return". The parables of the Kingdom began with the concept of sowing and the metaphor dominates the earlier parables on which we have dwelt in detail. The metaphor of Kingdom service presented in this last parable is that of trade. Perhaps our normal habits of thought encourage a discreditable view of trading, but there are other sides which should be prominent in our thoughts of this parable. Spurgeon has a stirring sermon on this parable, and especially on the request to trade. "I dare say they might have been inclined to argue, 'Our master's cause is assailed, let us fight for him' : yet he did not say 'fight', but 'trade'. Peter drew his sword. Oh, yes, we are eager combatants, but slow merchants."

"The work he prescribed was one that would bring them out. Trade develops a man's perseverance, patience and courage; it tests honesty, truthfulness and firmness. It is a singularly excellent discipline for character. When this nobleman gave his servant the pound, it was that he might see what stuff he was made of. Trade with small capital means personal work and drudgery, long hours and few holidays; plenty of disappointments and small gains".

Creditable trade meets human need. Where would any country be without those who find their livelihood in providing food, clothing and housing? Trading with the Lord's pound meets human need in its most profound form, the spiritual. It brings light in darkness, life in place of death, tranquil peace in place of anxiety, hope instead of despair, and security within the veil. Trade was, in this case, their selection ground for ruling. In setting them to trade, the nobleman was selecting those suitable to rule in his kingdom. "For, see, when he came to the man who had earned ten pounds, he gave him ten cities! There is no proportion between the poor service and the rich reward. A pound is rewarded with a city. The rewards of the millennium will evidently be all of grace, because they are so incomparably beyond anything which the servant's earning could have deserved."

Notice also the implication that there was power in the pound. "Thy pound hath gained ten pounds." The hint is that the pound possessed a dynamic of its own. And we have only to cast our mind back to the power of the Word entrusted to the sower to see how the different figures unite with each other.

"**Till I come.**" The parable has perforce to pass over the fact that the end-point in this service for the majority of individuals who have engaged in it has been death, by which they have passed into the immediate presence of the waiting Saviour. Nevertheless the parable does present the Second Advent as both the end point for the service as a whole, and also the hope which animates each servant throughout the period of the Lord's absence.

This is a thought on which we must pause and gather together other cases in which the words 'till He come' have special power for disciples in these late times. Our lot is cast in sombre times. Iniquity abounds and the love of many waxes cold. The contrast is stark between the bright early days and the aspect which Christendom now presents. Then, the disciples did all things 'with one accord'. Now, the great house of 2 Timothy 2:20 is a present reality, with its utter confusion of vessels to honour and vessels to dishonour. The company which bears the Name of Christ marching with banners across the stage of the publicity media and the affairs of nations bears the plainest marks of the approaching apostasy. Those who truly cleave to His Word and Name present so obscure an aspect, and are so much in reproach. Is it conceivable that among the dimly discernible vestiges of a Bible Christianity, we should find it a viable proposition to continue steadfastly with the purpose to make good the commandments of the Lord? In the most explicit answer to this question, and in full knowledge of the obscurity and confusion which would come to pass in the last days, the Lord in His mercy has marked out certain aspects of life and service by attaching to them the marker light of this pertinent phrase, 'till I come'. By this He has left us in no possible doubt that we are to continue in and with these essentials to the end.

(1) "If I will that he tarry **till I come**, what is that to thee?" (John 21:22) The disciple is to act on the absolute certainty that the Lord is disposing the lives of His own people individually — For how long? — until He comes. Here gleams the personal relation of the Lord to the totality of the life of each individual disciple. (Here is the true existentialism — a human life

in its totality). Every manifold detail of the life of each disciple depends simply and solely on this phrase, "If I will" No confusion, no darkness, no futility, exists in the realm, "If I will". There, is only peace, light, certainty, and victory.

(2) "For as often as ye eat this bread, and drink this cup, ye do show the Lord's death **till He come**." (1 Corinthians 11:26) The second direction bearing the marker light refers to the central ordinance of Christianity, the Lord's Supper. In each of the synoptic Gospels are recorded sayings of the Lord connecting the institution of the Supper with the Kingdom. "I will drink no more of the fruit of the vine, until that day that I drink it new in the kingdom of God." (Mark 14:25). "I will not drink of the fruit of the vine, until the kingdom of God shall come". (Luke 22:18). It is perhaps significant that this is one of the cases in which Matthew does not use 'the Kingdom of heaven'. "I will not drink henceforth of this fruit of the vine, until that day when I drink it new with you in my Father's kingdom." (Matthew 26:29). In a mysterious way these phrases seem to assign a place to the Supper to fill the whole amount of time until the coming of the Kingdom.

(3) Finally, the marker lights also the service commanded in our parable, "Occupy **till I come**". It is most remarkable that this last of the parables of the Kingdom of God should so clearly answer the vital questions determining a true understanding of the Kingdom, and of a fitting response. Have we been correct in making so much of the two forms of the Kingdom, the present and the future? Indeed we have. The parable proclaims inescapably that the period of the future Kingdom, with the presence of the King, is preceded by a period when His authority is acknowledged and acted on by a few in the midst of His enemies. Have we been justified in insisting on a yet future earthly Kingdom of God? Most certainly we have. The Kingdom and the cities over which the faithful servants rule, is in the same place where they say, "We will not have this man to reign over us". "The saints shall judge the world". (1 Corinthians 6:2) Have we rightly understood that the Second Advent of Christ is the moment of passing from the one form to the other? Unquestionably it is so. "When he returned" is the dividing point in the parable (v.15) between their serving Him in His absence, and their reigning with Him in His presence.

In the towering enterprise to which we have put our hand in terms of the present and future forms of the Kingdom of God, there is a vital confronting of the challenge of our times. In particular, **revolution** is the very air breathed in our age, and we must reckon with it. The first preachers of Christ's gospel were charged with being revolutionaries. "These that have turned the world upside down." (Acts 17:6) If this charge of revolutionary activity had been proceeded with, would they have been acquitted? It must be made perfectly clear that the New Testament promotes no kind of **political** revolution, and in particular prohibits absolutely any kind of violence. But there is an important sense in which a true revolutionary aim is fulfilled in

Christianity, and in the Kingdom of God. Gallons of ink and reams of paper have been expended on expositions of the revolutionary platform, not beginning with Karl Marx and certainly not ending with earnest current writings on revolutionary guerilla tactics. But the revolutionary platform in itself is not complicated. It has three planks. First, that current society is insupportably unjust, corrupt, and built on false values. Second, that it must be overthrown, often by violence. Thirdly, a new society must be built, purged from the rottenness of the old, and providing a setting for the good life for the masses of mankind. With the first item a Bible view of the societies of our times, as well as of the ancient societies, is to a large extent at one. Our reading of the Sermon on the Mount has underlined some of the false values which are the supports of modern societies. We must accept in large measure the destructively critical views of our society widely current, especially among angry youth.

Passing to the third plank, our faith shines certain and clear. We are not ashamed of the fact that, for the Church, our hope is set on "better things above" where Christ sits at the right hand of God. As for the world, we know with certainty, that when the Kingdom of God arrives with the Second Coming of Christ, the society which fulfils the "desire of all nations", in which the just aspirations of all mankind will be satisfied, will come into existence. Our faith, strong, clear and certain, is in One who possesses the power to put down all evil, the compassion which feels the sufferings of men through the ages, the instant mastery over all the calamities which have tormented man, and has laid the foundations in righteousness by the sacrifice of Calvary. To overthrow existing society is an enterprise to which the New Testament gives the Christian no kind of sanction, but on the contrary, expressly forbids it. The overthrow which is inevitable is reserved for the personal intervention of Christ at His coming. In the parable of the pounds, they were to trade, not to fight. Spreading the present interest of the absent master, and not revolution, was the work commanded.

The nature of the Christian's objective in the present, compared with the second plank in the revolutionary platform, is a matter of the highest importance. The revolutionaries of the New Left are highly dissatisfied with previous revolutions, because they have not removed the faults of the old societies. In place of oppressive privilege of the few, they have brought about a society with more oppressive privilege for a different few, and the Christian can see the reason. No revolution without God can conceivably get to the root of the matter, which is evil in the nature and practice of man. What is necessary is nothing less than revolution within individual men and women, in heart and mind, life and action. This kind of revolution is uniquely achievable through the gospel of Christ, and this is the nature of the enterprise to which Christians are called in the Kingdom of God. This is the seed-sowing, this is the trading, into which we are called to cast our energies under the Lordship of Christ.

Therefore our watchwords are to wait and to work: towards the **future** of the Kingdom of God, the positive, active, vigorous response which the Bible calls waiting; for the **present** enterprise of the Kingdom of God, to labour and to pray for it, knowing that in the present and in the future, the whole counsel of God is assured.

APPENDIX

An enormous literature has grown up on the Kingdom of God. In the twentieth century this has taken the form of a reaction against nineteenth century liberalism, which saw the Kingdom of God as a gradual amelioration of the world. In place of this view has been placed a recognition of the Kingdom as a dramatic intervention of God which would destroy the world order. The names of principal authors of this literature in the twentieth century are Johannes Weiss, Albert Schweitzer, C.H. Dodd, and Rudolph Bultmann. A general Christian reader of the present book, as distinct from a person familiar with theological literature, might well be looking over his shoulder all the time, and enquiring in what relation this book stands to that literature.

In the first place, of course, this book is not written by a professional theologian, and for this reason it is easier to write this appendix, since nothing here said will cause the slightest concern to the very eminent authors named. It will be found that in this book the work of these scholars is ignored. The reason for this omission is not that these works have not been read, but because the author, in common with evangelical Christians generally, decisively rejects a determining principle on which this literature is built. The purpose of this appendix is not to dispute the principle, but simply to bring it into the open. Otherwise the general Christian reader might easily overlook it, because he does not immediately grasp the real meaning of the euphemisms employed in the theological jargon. The principle in question is that these authors feel at liberty to alter, and in particular to omit, or ignore the words of Scripture, on the ground of literary and historical considerations. In this sense, these works belong to the "critical" school. In this sense the present book is unashamedly non-critical. It accepts the words of Scripture as the words of God.

Our first quotations are from Schweitzer, "The Mystery of the Kingdom of God", first published in 1901. On p.107/8 he deals with the parable of the sower and the following sentence occurs, "The detailed interpretation of the description of this loss, and the application to particular classes of men, as it lies before us in Mk4:13-20, is the product of a later view.." In other words, that Jesus supplied a detailed interpretation of the parable does not accord with Dr Schweitzer's views. He therefore eliminates it in the sense that he reasons from the passage as though the explanation were not there. On pp. 180/1 he takes out the Transfiguration and re-inserts it in a place which is dictated by "literary evidence". The subject of Jesus' use of the title "Son of Man" occupies pp. 194/6, and on 195/6 we have, "Hence all the passages are unhistorical in which, prior to Caesarea Philippi...he designates himself as Son of Man". This judgment is made on "critical and philological" grounds, and bluntly means they are not true and can be ignored.

Coming next to C.H. Dodd, I quote from "The Parables of the Kingdom", first published 1935 and revised 1961. In this author we are struck by a first appearance of understanding in Scriptural matters, which might easily mislead the reader. This first appearance is soon dispelled. At an early stage, (p.2) we meet the parable of the sower again. "Yet it must be confessed that the gospels themselves give encouragement to this allegorical method of interpretation. Mark interprets the parable of the Sower, and Matthew those of the Tares and the Drag-net, on just such principles; and both attribute their interpretation to Jesus Himself." So far so good. But does this mean that since the method appears in the Gospels in the mouth of the Lord it is unquestionably to be accepted? Not a bit of it! "It was the great merit of Adolph Jülicher, in his Die Gleichnisreden Jesu (1899-1910) that he applied a thoroughgoing criticism to this method, and showed,..that the attempts of the evangelists themselves to apply it rest on a misunderstanding". Thus, Dodd's conclusion in this sentence is that the evangelists (that is, the inspired authors of the Gospels) were mistaken in attempting to interpret these parables. To Mark's interpretation of the parable of the Sower in Mark 4:14-20 Dodd applies tests of language, style and vocabulary and concludes, "these facts create at once a presumption that we have here not a part of the primitive tradition of the words of Jesus, but a piece of apostolic teaching". By this setting in opposition of the "primitive tradition" and later "apostolic teaching", the fact of plenary inspiration vanishes.

Again, Dodd gives a first appearance of accepting that Scripture teaches both a present form and also a yet future form of the Kingdom of God. "In Jewish usage contemporary with the gospels we may distinguish two main ways in which the Kingdom of God is spoken of."

"First, God is King of His people Israel, and His kingly rule is effective in so far as Israel is obedient to the divine will...In this sense "The Kingdom of God" is a present fact."

"But in another sense "The Kingdom of God" is something yet to be revealed. God is more than King of Israel; He is King of all the world....Israel..looks forward to the day when 'The saints of the Most High shall take the kingdom,' and so the kingship of God will become effective over the whole world". (p.22) "The apocalyptic predictions of a future, and final, manifestation of the sovereign power of God are echoed... in such sayings as Mk.9:1..." What becomes of these predictions in the Gospels in Dodd's further development? They come to nothing. What does he think of Daniel, and the visions examined in detail in our earlier chapters? It all evaporates in a cloud of words about apocalyptic and eschatology, and we are left with this; "in Mark 14:62 the coming of the Son of Man with clouds, standing, as in Daniel, for the ultimate triumph of the cause of God, should have its historical counterpart in events immediately impending (as implied in the language of the Gospels), and these can hardly be other than the sacrificial death and resurrection of Christ". Why can they "hardly be other"? Only, so far as one can see, because the writer has already, on some ground undisclosed, decided that detailed prediction of events in the distant future are unacceptable. He continues, (p.83), "But these future tenses are only an accomodation of language. There is no coming of the Son of Man in history "after" His coming in Galilee and Jerusalem..." At the end of the book, (p.169), "We have, it appears, no warrant in the teaching of Jesus for affirming that the long cycle of history will lead inevitably to a millennial "Kingdom Come" on earth".

The general Christian reader might not recognise for what they are these jargon-phrases, "not historical", and "not a primitive tradition". They mean that the passages so described can be ignored, and so far as any value they may have for determining truth is concerned, they can be eliminated. Any thought of absolute reliance on divine truth revealed in words for our reverent submission in Daniel, the Gospels, and in the whole of Scripture, is scornfully rejected by this school.

From the point of view of the Bible Christian, of course, Bultmann is much worse. Once again there is the appearance of accepting a challenge in Scripture to the will of man which demands decision. God meets us in His word. *But*, it has been gathered from Butlmann's writings that when his process of demythologising is completed the content of the Christian faith has lost all substance, including the deity of Christ, His substitutionary death on the cross, His resurrection from the dead and His future return.

The essential basis of this literature, therefore, includes the application to the Bible of 'criticism' which is incompatible with acceptance of its *verbal* inspiration. There is indeed to be criticism, but the ground taken in this book is that all the words of man, all the results of his reason must be brought under the criticism of the Word of God, the Bible. "The word of God is living, and powerful.. and is a critic of the thoughts and intents of the heart." (Hebrews 4:12). It is for us, therefore, to submit ourselves to God's words in Scripture in all matters of faith and action.

INDEX of SUBJECTS

Abraham	11
Affliction	45f
Age. End of the,	40, 64 - 66, 77 - 79, 97f
A-Millennialism	22f
Antioch in Pisidia	50f, 58
Ananias and Sapphira	84
Anxiety	3f, 46f
Archelaus	112
Augustine	22, 23, 25
Augustus	112
Babylon	67
Beast	23
Bede	81
Binding and Loosing	83f
Bultmann	120, 122
Calvin.	22
Characters valued in Society	32f, 91 - 93
Chesterton. G.K.,	4, 34
Church	71, 74f, 81 - 86
Cities addressed by Paul	7
Colman	81
Communism	2
Constantine	67
Cornelius	53f, 55f, 61
Counsel. Eternal,	102
Cousin. Mrs A.R.,	99
Critical Theology	100, 120 - 122
Cross	74, 75, 91, 147
David	19
Democratic Elections	26
Devil	45, 65, 67
Disarmament	26
Discourses in Matthew	6, 31 - 36, 38 - 79, 97 - 102
Dodd. C.H.,	120 - 122

Ecumenical Movement	67, 69
Edersheim	84
Elijah	90
Ephesian Elders	7f
Ephesus	7, 51
Epicurus	47
Establishment	67
Ethiopian Eunuch	53, 55
Ezra	72
Father (in Heaven)	2, 3, 31, 47, 64, 66, 79, 82f, 91
Flesh	107f
Forgiveness	92
Foundation	83
Foundation of the World	102
Fruit	12, 108
Galileo	43, 45
Gospel	56, 58, 106
Gospel of the Kingdom	10, 77f, 97f, 101f
Grant. F.W.,	71, 77
Hedonism	47
Herod Agrippa I	50
Herod the Great	112
Hole. F.B.,	85
Holy Spirit	12, 13, 31, 100, 107f
Humility	92
Inheriting the Kingdom	8, 106 - 108
Instantaneous Conversion	52f
Inter-Advent Period	64, 71
Iona	81
Israel	11f, 71 - 74
Jerusalem Council	85
John the Baptist	11
Jonson. Ben,	59
Judgment of the Dead	101
Judgment of Living Nations	101
Keys. The power of the	83f
Kingdom of God and Kingdom of Heaven compared	12 - 14

Kingdom of God no existence before N.T.	10 - 12
Kings of the North and of the South	57
Knox. John..	22
Law ..	.32, 33 - 36
Leaven	68f
Loosing. Binding and,	83, 84
Losing our lives	90f
Loyola. Ignatius,	60
Luther	56
Lydia..	53
Manoah	82
Marxism	2, 118
Midnight Cry	99, 100
Millennium ..	10f, 25 - 28, 89f, 116
Milton	59
Moses	11, 59, 90, 91, 114f
Mountain Top Experiences	91
Mysteries	6, 11, 38 - 41
Nature of the Kingdom ..	8, 106, 108
Nebuchadnezzar ..	12, 18, 19, 22, 26
Northumbria. Kingdom of,	81
Organisation	55, 58

Parables:	Foolish Virgins	99 - 101
	Household Servants	99
	Husbandmen (wicked) ..	93
	Labourers in the Vineyard	93
	Leaven in Meal	68 - 69
	Marriage of the King's Son	93
	Mustard Seed	66 - 68
	Net cast into Sea ..	77 - 79
	Pearl ..	74 - 75, 83
	Pounds	112 - 117
	Rich Fool	3
	Sheep and Goats ..	101 - 102
	Sower..	43 - 49, 50
	Tares ..	64 - 66
	Treasure hid in Field	71 - 74

Paul	7f, 50, 57, 53, 54, 56, 61
Permissive Society.	107
Peter	54, 56, 61, 81 - 85, 89 - 91
Pharisees	83
Philip	51, 55
Philippi	53
Pleasure	47f
Popes: Gregory I and Gregory VI	67
Power	108
Prayer	3, 4, 47, 61f
Preaching the Word	43, 44, 49, 50 - 62
Rapture of the Saints	98 - 101, 116, 117
Reformers	99
Remnant. Jewish,..	97, 98
Resurrection of Christ	51f, 105
Resurrection of the Saints	105
Revolution	68, 117, 118
Rewards	116
Rich Young Ruler	92f
Riches	47
Righteousness, Peace and Joy	108 - 110
Rock	81, 83
Rome. Church of,	67, 69, 81, 85
Roman Empire	10, 23, 98
Rutherford. Samuel,	99f
Sanctification	60f
Saul of Tarsus	53
Schweitzer. Albert,	120f
Second Coming	8, 11, 21 - 24, 40, 97 - 101, 116f
Separation	99
Sleep. Spiritual,	65, 100f
Solomon	11f, 19
Son of the Living God	82
Son of Man	22, 23, 64, 66, 71, 74, 79, 82
Sonship. Christ's, ..	89
Spurgeon	49, 115
Stone	19, 20
Strikes	2

Supper. The Lord's, ... 117

Temptation.. 45
Ten Tribes 73
Times of the Gentiles 19
Trading 115f
Transfiguration .. .. 89 - 91
Tree 66f
Trench. R.C., ... 112
Tribulation. The Great, ... 98
Tyrannus 51

Values 3
Vespasian 23, 67

Weak and the Strong 108
Wesley. John, ... 52f
Whitby. Council of, ... 81
Wilfrid 81
Witness 99
Word. Preaching the, ... 43, 44, 49, 50 - 62
Worry 3f, 46f

INDEX of SCRIPTURES

Genesis
4: 23 — 34
49: 24 — 19

Exodus
19: 5 — 72

Deuteronomy
14: 2 — 72
26: 18, 19 — 72

Judges
13: 6 and 22 — 82

1 Chronicles
28: 5 — 11, 19

Psalms
2: 7, 8 — 20, 89
8: 4 - 8 — 82
16: 11 — 48
19: 7 - 14 — 191
21: 4 — 20
51: 10 — 60
66: 18 — 60
72: 14 - 19 — 28
92 — 109
96 - 99 — 109
118: 22 — 19
122: 6 — 75
137: 5, 6 — 75

Canticles
5: 2 — 101

Isaiah
2: 3, 4 — 10, 26, 27
5: 1 - 7 — 12
8: 6 — 21
:14 — 19
9: 6, 7 — 20, 28
11: 10 - 13 — 73
25 - 27 — 109
25: 9 — 10
 : 2, 15 - 18 — 21
28: 16 — 19, 83
32 — 109
42: 1 - 4 — 21, 113f
51: 1, 2 — 20
54: 7 - 10 — 73f
66 — 109

Jeremiah
2: 2 — 72

Ezekiel
29: 30 — 19
30: 24 - 26 — 19

Daniel
2: 31 - 45 — 15, 18 - 22
 : 35 — 12
 : 44 — 10, 18
7: 2 - 27 — 15 - 18, 22 - 24
 : 13 — 22, 23

Hosea
3: 4 - 5 — 73

Joel
2: 28 - 32 — 27

Zephaniah
3: 17 — 74

Zechariah
13: 7 — 20

Matthew
4: 17 — 13
5, 6, 7 — 6, 29 - 36
5: 1 - 16 — 32, 33
 : 17 - 48 — 32, 33 - 36
6: 33 — 14
8: 11 — 38
8, 9 — 39
9: 36 — 39

10: 5 - 23	97	4: 15	45
13	6, 37 - 49, 63 - 79	: 19	46
13: 3 - 8 & 19 - 23	42 - 49	9: 1	89
: 11	38	14: 25	117
: 11 - 16	37, 39 - 41	Luke	
: 24 - 30 & 36 - 43	63 - 69	7: 28	9, 11, 13
: 31, 32	13	8: 12	45
: 33	13, 63, 68f	: 14	46, 48
: 35	102	9: 27	89
: 37	78	: 31	93
: 44 - 46	70 - 75	11: 52	83
: 44	70 - 74	12: 13 - 31	11
: 47 - 50	76 - 78	13: 20 - 21	13
: 45, 46	74, 75	16: 13	47
: 52	41	: 16	9, 11, 13
16: 13 - 19	80 - 86	19: 11 - 17	111 - 119
: 18	83, 85	21: 25, 26	78
: 21 - 24	90	22: 18	117
: 28	87, 89	John	
17: 1 - 8	87 - 91	3: 3 & 5	13
18: 4	87, 91f	10: 16	75
: 23 - 35	87, 92	13: 10	59f
19: 23 - 24	14, 88, 92f	16: 12 - 13	31
21: 33 - 43	93	17: 11, 21, 22	75
: 43	11, 12, 14	: 17 - 19	60
: 44	21	: 24	102
22: 1 - 14	93	21: 22	116
23: 13	83	Acts	
24, 25	6, 95 - 102	1: 3	7
24: 1 - 44	95, 97 - 99	2: 16 - 21	27
: 14	17	4: 2 and 33	61
: 27	21	6: 7	50
: 30, 31	11, 23, 73	: 4 - 6	61
: 45 - 25: 30	6, 99	8: 5, 14	51
: 45 - 51	99	: 15	61
25: 1 - 13	95, 96, 99 - 101	9: 11	61
: 14 - 30	114f	: 30	56
: 31 - 46	6, 69, 101 - 102	: 40	61
26: 29	117	10: 2, 30	53, 61
Mark		: 9	61
1: 14, 15	9 - 13		

11: 25	56	Ephesians	
12: 5	61	1: 3	32
: 24	50	:4	102
13: 2	56	5: 5	8, 107
: 3	61	:25, 26	74
: 49	50	Phillippians	
15	85	4: 6	3f
15: 7	84	Colossians	
: 40	7	3: 23, 24	47
16: 12 - 40	7	4: 11	8, 103, 106
: 25	61	1 Thessalonians	
17: 1 - 9	7	2: 12	8, 103, 106
: 3	51	4: 15 - 18	98
: 18	47, 52	5: 10	100f
18: 1 - 28	7	: 23	60
: 29 - 19: 41	7	2 Thessalonians	
19: 20	50	1: 5	8, 103, 105
20: 17 - 38	7f	1 Timothy	
28: 8	61	6: 9, 10, 17 - 19	47
23, 31	8	2 Timothy	
Romans		2: 14 - 21	43, 58
7: 15 - 23	107	3: 4	48
8: 32	74	Titus	
14: 17	8, 104, 108 - 110	3: 3	45
1 Corinthians		Hebrews	
3: 12 - 17	84	10: 10	60
4: 20	8, 104, 108	11: 24, 25	48
5	84	James	
6: 9, 11	8, 103, 106, 107	4: 1 - 3	48
10: 32	79, 97, 101	1 Peter	
11: 26	107	1: 2	60
13: 10 - 12	26	: 3	32
15: 24 - 28	103, 105	: 19, 20	102
: 50	8, 103, 106	2: 3 - 8	19f, 83, 84
2 Corinthians		5: 7	3
7: 1	60		
Galatians			
2: 20	35		
5: 21	8, 104, 107		

2 Peter			5: 9	75
1: 11, 12, 16 - 19	90		12: 10	8
2: 1	74		13: 1	23, 78
Revelation			14: 6	77
1: 5	75		17: 3 - 18	23
			20: 1 - 6	22, 25
			: 12	101

www.ingramcontent.com/pod-product-compliance
Lightning Source LLC
Chambersburg PA
CBHW020007050426
42450CB00005B/354